How To Be An Effective Litigation Consultant And Expert Witness

Budd J. Hallberg

authorHOUSE®

AuthorHouse™
1663 Liberty Drive
Bloomington, IN 47403
www.authorhouse.com
Phone: 1-800-839-8640

© *2010 Budd J. Hallberg. All rights reserved.*

No part of this book may be reproduced, stored in a retrieval system, or transmitted by any means without the written permission of the author.

First published by AuthorHouse 7/21/2010

ISBN: 978-1-4490-9934-3 (e)
ISBN: 978-1-4490-9933-6 (sc)

Printed in the United States of America
Bloomington, Indiana

To my best friend and wife,
Diana

Contents

Acknowledgments ix

Preface xi

Introduction xiii

I. Industries Most in Need of Expert Witnesses 1

II. Representing the Plaintiff or Defendant 7

III. Litigation Forums 11

IV. Experience Required 17

V. Marketing Your Credentials 21

VI. Compensation 29

VII. Curriculum Vitae 33

VIII. Engagement Letter 41

IX. Expert Report 45

X. Peer Review 49

XI. Giving a Deposition 55

XII. Tales from the Hot Seat 59

XIII. Conclusion 69

Epilogue 77

Appendices 83

Glossary of Selected Terms 108

Bibliography 115

Index 119
About The Author 125

Acknowledgments

Over the years, I've had the privilege of providing litigation support and expert witness consultant services to the following financial institutions, law firms and organizations. Their trust and confidence made the preparation and completion of this book possible. They are: the Federal Deposit Insurance Corporation (Washington, D.C.), Gusrae, Kaplan & Bruno (New York), Lambert & Weiss (New York), Gerald B. Lefcourt, Esq. (New York), Merrill Lynch Pierce Fenner & Smith (New York), the New York Stock Exchange (New York), Perkins Coie (Seattle), Proskauer Rose (Los Angles), Reed Smith Shaw & McClay (Washington, D.C.), Rosch & Ross (Houston), Sidley Austin, Brown & Wood (Chicago), Smith Barney, Inc. (New York) and Sutherland, Asbill & Brennan (Washington, D.C.).

I want to express my gratitude to V. Bruce Hirshauer, Ph.D. (Johns Hopkins University in Baltimore, Maryland), a colleague and friend, who reviewed this manuscript and provided me with valuable criticism. I am appreciative to Tom Joyce, Ph.D. (Georgetown University in Washington, D.C.) who examined the essay for philosophical thought and completeness.

I am grateful to Raymond C. Speciale, Esq., CPA, an aviation law attorney who makes frequent use of experts in practice. He is a professor of law and accounting at Mount Saint Mary's University in Emmitsburg, Maryland. I wish to give sincere thanks to Susannah J. Wakefield, Esq., who provided legal insights into many facets of the essay. She has practiced law in London, New York and Bermuda. Her work includes international commercial litigation and arbitration.

Budd J. Hallberg

Preface

You have likely purchased this book for one of four reasons. First, you have expertise in a particular field and are considering whether you should use that expertise in some capacity as a litigation consultant or expert witness. Second, you have already made the decision to try your hand at litigation consulting, but have been unsuccessful - no lawyer has called you to seek your services. Third, you purchased this book because you were engaged by a lawyer to testify in a matter as an expert witness and had a bad experience. Either your deposition went poorly or your performance at trial was less than stellar. A fourth reason might be, you are currently a successful litigation consultant and expert witness and are just curious to read what one of your colleagues has to say about the subject. Whatever your reason may be for acquiring the book, I hope that you find the text will add value to your career as a litigation consultant.

Introduction

If it is any comfort to you, at one time or another -

Every expert witness has given a bad deposition or testified poorly at trial.

All experts have had less than a stellar day in the courtroom. However, if a person expects to sustain a career long-term as a litigation consultant, those types of occurrences can't happen too often. That is why it is important that some successes be achieved early to provide a fall-back position upon which an expert can use to rebuild.

Litigation Consultants **and** ***Expert Witnesses*** **can't afford to have many setbacks at deposition or trial. Word gets around quickly as to who is good and not so good in the courtroom.**

Most of the litigation consultant's business is built on referrals. It is important that a litigation consulting career be constructed on a solid foundation.

For those who make the decision to go forward and build a litigation consulting practice, this book is designed as a guide to how they may best draw on their experience and effectively market their credentials to the legal community. You will learn how to establish a litigation consulting and expert witness fee schedule for services rendered.

The text describes the necessary information required to be included in an expert witness's Curriculum Vitae. A sample Curriculum Vitae is provided in Appendix B. The elements which should be included in a litigation Engagement Letter are explained in Chapter VIII and displayed for easy reference in Appendix C. Finally and most important, you will be taught how to prepare an Expert Report and have that report peer reviewed. A sample Expert Report is shown in Appendix D. You will be given specific guidance on how to give effective testimony at deposition or trial.

The primary goal of this book is to provide guidance as to how the litigation process works, the role of the litigation

consultant or non-testifying expert and how a testifying expert witness fits overall into the legal paradigm.

The reader is provided with an extensive glossary of terms toward the end of the book. This will better enable the successful navigation of a broad range of litigation topics discussed in the text.

Please note there are three terms which are used extensively throughout the text. They are: litigation consultant, non-testifying expert and expert witness. Two of these terms, litigation consultant and non-testifying expert, are often interchangeable. Expert witness or testifying expert means one who will be giving a deposition and intends to testify at trial. Also to be noted, the term *litigation* applies equally to arbitration as well as court actions.

Finally, the book discusses a number of pitfalls to which experts are exposed. It goes on to indicate how best to avoid those deadly minefields. The principles developed here are based on twenty-three years of hardened personal experience.

Chapter I

Industries Most in Need of Expert Witnesses

Laws and institutions must go hand in hand with the progress of the human mind.

-Thomas Jefferson

While nearly any service or business transaction could possibly end up in a lawsuit, there are some industries that tend to be more prone to litigation and arbitration than others. If you have experience in any of these targeted industry groupings, you will want to make known to the legal community your particular field of expertise and willingness to act as a litigation consultant and expert witness in that area. The industries most in need of expert witnesses include: 1) construction, 2) medicine, 3) securities, 4) commodity futures, 5) internet and telecommunications, 6) real estate and 7) corporate America.

The **construction** industry attracts the lion's share of arbitration matters handled by the American Arbitration Association (AAA).[1] The function of AAA is more fully described in Chapter III. Plaintiff filings include allegations such as: 1) cost overruns, 2) failure to meet specifications, 3) labor disputes, and 4) personal injury matters.

Clearly, the **medical** field is a targeted profession. It seems to draw more than its fair share of lawsuits. Large numbers of medical malpractice lawsuits are filed annually in America. While some medical malpractice lawsuits are frivolous, there are a number of cases whereby medical professionals have erred in ways leaving patients non-functional for the remainder of their lives.

The target audience for medical field lawsuits includes: 1) hospitals, 2) doctors and 3) medical support staff. Allegations range from failure of hospital internal controls and procedures to negligent behavior by

---

1 Appendix E.

medical professionals. Incidents include: 1) mismatching of newborns with their rightful mothers, 2) permanent brain damage to patients as a result of improper dosages of anesthesia administered by the anesthesiologist during surgery and 3) surgeons who removed the wrong foot during an amputation, leaving patients permanently immobile.

Wall Street continuously tries to 'rip off' the public.

Another targeted group is the **securities** and **commodity futures** industry. Because of the global financial crisis and its impact on world economies, this industry and the demand for litigation consultants and expert witnesses is discussed in greater detail in Appendix A.

Goldman Sachs is a premier Wall Street investment banking and securities firm. Gary Gensler "was co-head of finance at (that organization) and one of the youngest partners in the history of the firm."[2] In 2008, he was named "to head the Commodity Futures Trading Commission ..."[3] In 2002, Mr. Gensler coauthored a book entitled *The Great Mutual Fund Trap*. "The cover of (the text) shows a faceless banker playing a shell game. Inside, Mr. Gensler warns investors that Wall Street is continuously trying to rip them off."[4] Wall Street bankers that 'rip off the public' may well be breaking the law.

Because personal financial assets are at stake, stock brokerage firms have for years been the subject of lawsuits by clients. Most claims focus on financial loss being attributable to misconduct by the firm's registered representative. That is to say, the financial loss was caused by the customer's account executive.

Customer lawsuits involving securities and commodity futures trading usually include allegations of: 1) unauthorized trading, 2) negligence, 3) churning and 4) an absence of corporate supervision of their account by the firm's compliance and administrative staff. Many of the claims filed allege that stockbrokers just outright stole their clients' money.

In March 2008, because of severe financial problems the investment firm "Bear Stearns ... agreed to be sold-for $2 a share" to JP Morgan

---

2   Baer, Gregory and Gensler, Gary. *The Great Mutual Fund Trap*. New York: Broadway Books, 2002, p. 336.
3   *The Economist*. A new sheriff. Washington, DC. September 5th-11th 2009, p. 83.
4   Ibid.

Chase.⁵ Founded in 1858, the investment banking firm Lehman Brothers became embroiled in credit default swaps and other exotic financial products involving real estate and leverage. In the fall of 2008, "the financial system came close to a breakdown" and events led to Lehman Brothers.⁶ The decision was made to "allow Lehman Brothers to fail."⁷

On October 11, 2007, the Dow Jones Industrial Average (DJIA) reached a high of 14,279. In December 2008, the DJIA would reach a low of 8,515. In other words, from its October 2007 high to the December 2008 low, the DJIA had lost over forty percent (40%) in value, and that's not even adjusted for inflation. That is to say, the financial meltdown of key Wall Street banking and investment institutions coupled with a severe stock market decline in 2008 ushered in the Great Recession of the 21ˢᵗ century (hereinafter the "Crash of 2008"). Since then, lawsuits alleging institutional wrongdoing have reached unprecedented levels.⁸

The commodity futures industry provides a place for commercial users of a product to hedge their cash market risk and for individuals and trading organizations to speculate on price movement. Because these markets are highly leveraged and because of the way they are structured, for over one hundred years, the commodity futures industry has been riddled with fraud.

Frank Norris (1870-1902) was an American novelist during the *Progressive Era*. In his book *The Octopus,* Norris writes of the beginning of this unseemly one hundred year period of fraud starting with the wheat scandals of the late 1800s.⁹ The shenanigans Norris speaks about have continued, on and off, from that time up through and including Wall Street's financial "Super-Bubble" which popped in 2008.¹⁰

The global financial meltdown is a result of the unbridled trading of exotic swap and derivative products.¹¹

---

5   Sorkin, Andrew Ross. *Too Big to Fail*. New York: Penguin Group, 2009, p. 10.
6   Soros, George. *The Crash of 2008 and What it Means*. New York: PublicAffairs, 2009, p. 161.
7   Ibid.
8   Ibid, p. 157.
9   Norris, Frank. *The Octopus*. Boston: Houghton Mifflin, 1958.
10   Soros, pp. 83-84.
11   Appendix A.

This development will increase demand for litigation consultants and expert witnesses who have knowledge of the mechanics and workings of these esoteric financial products. The monetary losses to date are in the trillions of dollars. The multiplicity of causal issues remains open with no immediate resolution in sight. This will provide litigation opportunities for years to come.

The **internet and telecommunications** industries are an emerging business grouping which is in demand for highly skilled technicians who can act as litigation consultants and provide expert witness testimony in complex matters involving computer science. Abusive use of the internet ranges from high school hackers to criminal activities including international terrorist organizations. The opportunities in this field are nearly endless.

The **real estate** industry, especially in the aftermath of the "U.S. Housing Bubble," is attracting large numbers of lawsuits.[12] Breach of contract is at the forefront of a number of these claims. Misrepresentation is a close second. Title clearances and boundary issues give rise to real estate litigation. Tax considerations are often associated with real estate transaction disputes as well. Most recently, a number of Wall Street banks and hedge funds are the object of inquiry as to their handling of "complex securities – known as synthetic collateralized debt obligations, or C.D.O.'s."[13] These are real estate mortgage related securities.

On December 24, 2009 a column written by Gretchen Morgenson and Louise Story appeared in the *New York Times* which reported that C.D.O.'s (traded by a number of Wall Street firms) are "… now the subject of scrutiny by investigators in Congress, at the Securities and Exchange Commission and at the Financial Industry Regulatory Authority, Wall Street's self-regulatory organization, according to people briefed on the investigations."[14] Tetsuya Ishikawa wrote a book entitled *How I Caused the Credit Crunch*. "In it, he said that bankers deserted their clients who had bought mortgage bonds when that market collapsed: 'We had moved on to hurting others in our quest for self-preservation'."[15]

---

12 Soros, pp. 84-93.
13 Morgenson, Gretchen and Story, Louise. <u>Banks Bundled debt, Bet Against It and Won.</u> *The New York Times*. December 24, 2009, p. A1.
14 Ibid.
15 Ibid, p. B4. Ishikawa, Tetsuya. *How I Caused the Credit Crunch*. London: Icon Books Ltd, 2009, p. 7.

Andrew Ross Sorkin is a columnist for the *New York Times*. In his book *Too Big to Fail*, he points out that the goal on Wall Street was to generate commissions and fees for themselves with a reckless disregard for their clients.[16] Litigation consultants with expertise in the mechanics and workings of these complex products will be in great demand in the years to come.

Corporate misconduct claims include: 1) age, gender and race discrimination issues associated with hiring and termination practices, 2) sexual harassment charges, 3) breach of employment contracts and 4) entitlement programs such as company health insurance plans and severance pay. These issues require litigation consultants who are experts in such areas as personnel and human resource management.

The above illustrations evidence the need for persons with highly specialized skills in areas requiring a specific expertise. The litigation consultant who has a command of her work discipline and who is able to articulate effectively complex issues to the average person seated on a jury can expect to be in great demand for litigation consultant and expert testimony work well into the 21st century.

---

16   Sorkin, p. 538.

Chapter II

Representing the Plaintiff or Defendant

Ei incumbit probatio qui dicit, non qui regat.[17]

At a minimum, a lawsuit must have one plaintiff and one defendant. More complicated cases, especially those involving large sums of money, will often have multiple plaintiffs and numerous defendants.

People who are defendants in criminal matters are presumed innocent until proven guilty. Defendants in civil matters are also presumed innocent until it is proven that they have somehow caused harm to another person. That being said, there seems to be something almost inherent in the American persona that quietly draws people (litigation consultants and jury members) toward the plaintiff. Although the reasoning is fallacious, people will conclude early on that something must have gone wrong somewhere; otherwise a lawsuit would not have been filed. This kind of thinking is even more prevalent when a federal government agency takes an action against a person or organization.

Professional litigation consultants want to utilize their expertise in a constructive way. They want to assist in the judicial process and see justice administered properly and fairly.

All too often we read of a tragedy whereby a patient went into surgery to have a foot amputated only later to find out that the surgeon amputated the wrong foot. The story of an elderly woman being fleeced out of her life savings by an unscrupulous stockbroker is heartbreaking. We hear of numerous building contractors who incurred cost overruns on construction projects and ended up being sued by the contracting party.

These happenings occur almost daily in America. Countless actions are archived in various litigation forums throughout the United States.

---

17   The burden of proof rests on who asserts, not on who denies.

Some cases receive a great deal of media attention. Most, however, go undetected. High profile cases will more likely have an impact upon litigation consultants and expert witnesses than low profile matters.

Cases which involve tragic happenings such as the legendary Lacy Peterson case or the Bernard Madoff scandal give rise to the need for litigation consultant and expert witness representation. In such instances, expert litigation consultants make a positive contribution to the litigation process by assisting the jury in understanding complicated matters associated with the case. For example, this might include such things as reading and understanding forensic studies. It could be an explanation of how to understand and interpret a certain piece of evidence.

I knew an Administrative Law Judge who worked for a federal government regulatory commission. His job was to hear customer complaints and enforcement actions filed against persons and organizations that were required to be registered with his agency. These registrants included futures commission merchant firms, introducing broker organizations and associated persons. One day the judge said to me, "The more of these cases I hear, the more I come to believe these matters should be captioned 'Mr. Greed *vs.* Mr. Chicanery'."

I gave serious thought to what the judge had to say. Upon reflection, I think that his remark suggests that neither side has a monopoly on virtue. That is to say, when seeking justice in resolving differences in a lawsuit, that oftentimes both the plaintiff and the defendant bear some responsibility for the happening. In other words, the truth is blurred and lies somewhere in the middle-the gray area.

Metaphorically, few things in life are crystal clear. The notion of justice as fairness begins to emerge. However, it must be kept in mind that when it comes to dispute resolution matters, there are no absolutes. No judicial system is perfect.

Defendants in a lawsuit are entitled equally to legal representation as *plaintiffs.*

Defendants frequently engage the services of a litigation consultant or expert witness to assist them with their case. This is typically done through the law firm who has been retained to represent the defendant in the matter.

The role of the expert witness is to bring to the table an expertise that will assist the fact finder (be that the judge, jury or arbitration panel) in arriving at a sound decision. You have an auxiliary role in the legal process. The expert witness must present her findings and give testimony in an impartial manner.

The true professional litigation consultant must be able to apply equally her expertise to both plaintiff and defendant matters.

In deciding whether to do plaintiff or defendant work, what it really boils down to is the individual case itself. Each lawsuit must be reviewed carefully and weighed on its own merits. If you feel uncomfortable with a particular litigant's position, you just pass on the opportunity.

Litigation consultants and expert witnesses should keep an open mind when deciding whether to accept plaintiff or defendant work. Always remember "For such law as a man gives another, He should himself obey it, by right ..."[18] First, if you are truly good at what you do, it would be a shame to deny either plaintiffs or defendants your expertise and talents in assisting them with their case. Second, from a professional point of view, it is critical that your credentials carry the label "professional," and to be professional, your work must not be biased. You must be impartial.

Judges tend to look favorably upon expert witnesses whose litigation resume is well balanced between plaintiff and defendant work.

This demonstrates neutrality and objectivity in case formulation. This later becomes evident when you make your oral presentation at the deposition hearing or while giving courtroom testimony. Third, expert witnesses who do work only for plaintiffs are often typecast as champions for *victim's rights*. Experts who concentrate on defendant work only are often labeled *bagmen* or *bagwomen* for industry. Either way, experts should avoid placing limitations on their professional credentials. You don't want to get trapped in this position.

Based on your evaluation of the merits of the case, do accept plaintiff and defendant work. Having a balanced litigation portfolio makes you a

---

18   Chaucer, Geoffrey. *The Canterbury Tales*. New York: Barnes & Noble Classics, 2006, p. 683.

valuable candidate to do expert witness work for the legal profession. It provides you with a sense of sincerity and objectivity. This will radiate when giving a deposition or oral testimony at a deposition hearing or trial.

Chapter III

Litigation Forums

> *Law is not justice and a trial is not a scientific inquiry into truth. A trial is the resolution of a dispute.*
>
> -Edison Haines

There are numbers of dispute resolution forums available to parties involved in lawsuits. These forums include: 1) reparations, 2) arbitration, 3) mediation and 4) courts - trials.

Alternative Dispute Resolution - Reparations

Headquartered in Washington, D.C., the U.S. Commodity Futures Trading Commission (CFTC) is "The Federal regulatory agency established by the CFTC Act of 1974 to administer the Commodity Exchange Act."[19] This agency has a "Reparations Program" which makes available an arbitration and court-like forum to hear cases. This venue is limited strictly to those persons who have suffered monetary injury as a result of alleged account mishandling by persons registered with the commission. Reparations provide opportunities for litigation consultant engagements and expert witness testimony.

Arbitration and Mediation

The American Arbitration Association (AAA) is the nation's leading provider of alternative dispute resolution services. General business and construction contract disputes are most often heard by AAA arbitration panels. Their national roster includes retired judges, attorneys and industry professionals. AAA has offices in all major cities throughout the United States. The International Centre for Dispute Resolution is

---

19   Office of Public Affairs: Commodity Futures Trading Commission. *The CFTC Glossary*. Washington, DC: CFTC Publications, 1992, p. 13 and Appendix E.

the international division of AAA. It is the world's leading provider of alternative dispute resolution services with an international roster comprised of lawyers and industry professionals.[20]

For the most part, securities disputes are resolved through mandatory arbitration. The Financial Industry Regulatory Authority (FINRA) operates the largest dispute resolution program for the securities industry in the United States. It handles nearly ninety percent of all securities arbitration claims filed involving clients of stock brokerage firms. FINRA handles disputes among brokerage firms as well as between brokerage firms and their employees. FINRA has office locations in Washington, D.C., San Francisco, Los Angeles, Chicago and Boca Raton, Florida.[21]

In the first eight months of 2009, "investors filed some 4,991 securities-arbitration claims."[22] These large numbers of filings are the result of the financial crisis of 2008. "Congress is considering eliminating mandatory arbitration, which would allow investors to take their complaints straight to court."[23] Whether it is an arbitration forum or a court setting, securities disputes provide lucrative opportunities for litigation consultants and expert witnesses who have a background in the securities field.

Headquartered in Chicago with an office in New York City, the National Futures Association (NFA) is registered by the CFTC as a futures association under the Commodity Exchange Act. NFA is a self-regulatory organization. It administers a nationwide arbitration and mediation program to handle disagreements between customers and futures trading professionals who are members of NFA.[24]

Arbitration provides opportunities for litigation consultant work and expert witness testimony. With respect to mediation, this is not the case. The role of the litigation consultant is dramatically reduced and would not include expert witness testimony.

In addition to administering a dispute resolution forum involving the public and business practitioners, except for AAA, the above

---

20 Appendix E.
21 Ibid.
22 Blumenthal, Robin G. Taking Aim at the Brokers. *Barron's*. October 19, 2009, p. 28.
23 Ibid.
24 Appendix E.

organizations have the capability to hear matters involving industry professionals as well as their own members. This is another area that often requires the need of a litigation consultant, especially one who has or has had industry experience.

For example, the U.S. Securities and Exchange Commission (SEC) regulations provide for the policing of the securities industry.[25] CFTC regulations provide for a similar activity, but only for the futures industry. After careful investigation, should the Director of the Division of Enforcement of either the SEC or CFTC conclude that a securities or futures registrant has violated a provision of the Securities Act or Commodity Exchange Act as the case may be; either agency could then take an enforcement action against the particular registrant-person, organization, or both. Actions may be brought in a court setting and heard before an administrative law judge who has been assigned to the agency by the Federal government's Office of Personnel Management.

As a self-regulatory organization (SRO), the NFA operates to maintain the integrity of the futures industry and to protect the public through effective oversight and policing of its members. Should the NFA discover that one of its members is operating outside of NFA rules, this SRO may take legal action against the member and have the case heard before a Business Conduct Committee (BCC) of NFA. Similar arrangements are in place at the SEC, FINRA, and at futures and securities exchanges. This evidences a growing need for professional litigation consultants and expert witnesses.

One comment about regulatory arbitration and enforcement action forums is important. All too often an industry criticism is that these forums are biased. The notion that hearing panels tend to favor the public, or in the case of internal industry differences, panels tend to lean toward the registrant organization bringing an action against one of their employees is prevalent. Having testified before arbitration hearing panels, and having sat on these panels as an industry representative, I have found this **not** to be the case. My recommendation is this: if after review, you feel comfortable in accepting a particular litigation assignment, do actively participate in industry sponsored arbitration hearings. First, this will broaden

---

25 Ibid.

your litigation resume and second, the action here is just as exciting as being in the courtroom.

There are a couple of things to keep in mind when testifying as an expert witness before an arbitration panel as opposed to testifying before a judge or jury. A jury is comprised of everyday folks drawn from the general public. Judges hear a myriad of cases involving a number of subjects. Neither a judge nor a jury will likely possess the industry knowledge which would comprise that of an arbitration panel. That is to say, in a courtroom setting the expert witness will often find her role to carry a dual responsibility. She will be required to act first as an educator and second, to provide testimony critical to a fair judicial outcome.

I offer these concluding remarks with respect to arbitration: I strongly suggest you consider making application to a number of the arbitration forums mentioned above and become an arbitration panelist. In doing so, you will accomplish three things. First, by sitting on a hearing panel and having first-hand knowledge, you will be able to dispel any notion of hearing panel bias. Second, by serving as an arbitrator, you will be able to observe other experts and take notice of their effectiveness. Third, the above experiences will enable you to sharpen your own skills as an expert witness.

Courts and Trials

The most challenging and exciting of all forums, of course, is the courtroom, especially if it is a jury trial. Court cases are classified as either civil or criminal. Civil cases are well structured with established procedures. This forum is most conducive to litigation consultant work. An expert report is required. Rehearsal of oral testimony to be given by the expert witness at trial is mandatory. Depending on the lawyers and judge involved, criminal trials can operate quite differently. Here, an *anything goes* environment may emerge and surprises can occur quite often. The expert witness has to be prepared for any eventuality.

In addition to finding the courtroom challenging, it can be one of the most rewarding experiences professionally. I was honored to have my testimony referred to in a judge's final decision. The judge said:

> ***"The Court in particular notes as helpful to its conclusion the testimony of the SHB Defendant's expert, Mr.***

> *Budd Hallberg. Mr. Hallberg was a very compelling and convincing witness relative to the COMEX, clearly knowledgeable of its procedures, rules and regulations, as well as those of the CFTC.*"[26]

These experiences not only enhance your credentials, but also provide critical insight with regard to the quality of your work. This kind of recognition is personally rewarding.

I have some comments about accepting litigation engagements involving criminal matters. Criminal cases are challenging and most demanding. They require much time and energy. The bar in criminal matters is raised high in comparison to civil cases. The reason for this is the degree of punishment that can be handed down by the judge. In criminal matters, a person can be sentenced to a life term in prison. A person can also be sentenced to death. That is not the case with civil proceedings.

Before you accept criminal litigation consultant work, let me make two points. First, read the case very carefully before you accept the assignment, and second, get retained and paid by the law firm making the representation. In fact, you should always receive your compensation from the law firm engaging your services, and not the named party in the case. This is especially true in criminal cases. The chief reason being, that it is most likely money will be at the heart of the matter and how the defendant came to acquire those funds will be at the core of the case. If you accept money directly from the defendant, it is possible you may be accepting ill-gotten funds for your work and later have to return some or all of the money you received. The notorious Bernard L. Madoff's $50 billion Ponzi scheme is a good illustration. By accepting consulting fee payments from the engaging law firm, the money you receive should be from *clean accounts*.

To avoid any professional conflicts or potential complications, you may wish to have your own attorney review the case and provide you with legal advice before accepting or rejecting a criminal assignment.

Accept litigation assignments in all *forums*.

---

26 Appendix F.

This broadens your experience and enhances your credentials as a litigation consultant and expert witness. It makes you more valuable to the litigation community and keeps you and your services in demand. Litigation forums, legal and regulatory reference listings are included in Appendix E.

Chapter IV

Experience Required

> *There are many truths of which the full meaning cannot be realized until personal experience has brought it home.*
>
> -John Stuart Mill

John Rawls (1921-2002) was professor of philosophy at Harvard University. He was the author of a number of works in moral and political philosophy. The "idea of a legal system" is logocentric to the idea of America. In his text, A *Theory of Justice,* Rawls posits by saying "I now wish to consider rights of the person as these are protected by the principle of the rule of law."[27] To better craft his arguments Rawls looks back to Immanuel Kant and Kant's "interpretation of *justice as fairness*."[28]

Immanuel Kant (1724-1804) "is one of the premier philosophers in the Western tradition."[29] His interpretation of the concept of justice is based on the notion of *autonomy*.[30] Kant argues that people "express their nature as free and equal rational beings subject to the general

---

27   Rawls, John. *A Theory of Justice*. Cambridge: Harvard University Press, 1971, p. 235. Footnote 20. For a general discussion, see Lon Fuller, *The Morality of Law* (New Haven, Yale University Press, 1964), ch. II. The concept of principal decisions in constitutional law is considered by Herbert Wechsler, *Principles, Politics, and Fundamental Law* (Cambridge, Harvard University Press, 1961). See Otto Kirchenheimer, *Political Justice* (Princeton, Princeton University Press, 1961), and J. N. Shklar, *Legalism* (Cambridge, Harvard University Press, 1964), pt. II, for the use and abuse of judicial forms in politics. J. R. Lucas, *The Principles of Politics* (Oxford, The Clarendon Press, 1966), pp. 106-143, contains a philosophical account.
28   Ibid, p. 251-257.
29   Pojman, Louis P. and Vaughn, Lewis. *Philosophy: The Quest for Truth*. New York: Oxford University Press, 2009, p. 495.
30   Rawls, *A Theory of Justice*, p. 251.

conditions of human life."[31] That is to say, "the lives of the saint and the scoundrel are equally the outcome of free choice and equally the subject of causal laws."[32] Rawls concludes by saying, "Thus justice as fairness is a theory of human justice and among its premises are the elementary facts about persons and their place in nature."[33]

In another of his texts, *Political Liberalism*, Rawls once again draws close attention to the notion of "justice as fairness."[34] Here, he explains his idea in terms of what he calls "the depth and breadth of an overlapping consensus…" [35] Rawls concludes by saying "…that the consensus goes down to the fundamental ideas within which justice as fairness is worked out."[36] That being said, "For although men know that they share a common sense of justice and that each wants to adhere to the existing arrangements, they may nevertheless lack full confidence in one another."[37]

A well credentialed expert witness can ease tension and reduce conflict in the litigation process. That is to say, she can fashion a doctrinal sense of justice as fairness to those engaged in the legal experience.

To qualify as an expert witness in a court of law or before an arbitration panel, a person must have a command of the mechanics and workings of a particular discipline. This would include: 1) hands-on industry experience, 2) academia or 3) federal or state government regulatory work.

During the litigation process, each party will consider whether it can get the other side's expert disqualified from testifying before the court or arbitration panel. As an alternative, each of the two counsels making representation, one for the plaintiff and the other for the defendant, will do their utmost to discredit the testimony of the other's expert.

It is critical that you are able to withstand this contest.

---

31   Ibid, 252-253.
32   Ibid, p. 254.
33   Ibid, p. 257.
34   Rawls, John. *Political Liberalism*. New York: Columbia University Press, 1996, p. 144.
35   Ibid, p. 149.
36   Ibid.
37   Rawls, *A Theory of Justice*, p. 240.

It is important that you indeed do possess the proper credentials to testify and that your testimony will provide valuable information to the jury or arbitration panel.

An expert witness with in-depth industry experience will often capture the attention of the jury or the arbitration panel early on. Of the three experiences mentioned above, **a strong industry background tends to provide the greatest credibility** and makes it difficult for most lawyers to cross-examine the expert successfully.

The next most recognizable source of experience is academia, especially if the expert displays a strong command of her academic discipline and achievement. Evidence of published works include: 1) books, 2) journal articles and 3) columns in recognized magazines and newspapers. Extensive speaking engagements and award recognition by industry peers are credential builders for the academic expert. Academic experts can be most difficult for lawyers to cross-examine effectively. There are, however, areas that make the academic expert vulnerable to courtroom ineffectiveness. The first area of exposure is where the academic is too cerebral and loses the jury during testimony. Without that touch of *boots-on-the-ground* experience, the academic often finds it challenging to deflect skillfully the inevitable 'hypothetical' question which is often asked by opposing counsel. Second, the person who brings to the table an elaborate set of academic credentials must keep in mind that her audience is not a Dissertation Review Board. For the most part, juries are comprised of everyday folks. Information needs to be imparted in such a fashion so that the non-technical person (each member of the jury) is able to understand your testimony. This will be less important if you are testifying before an arbitration panel which has at least one panelist who is an industry professional.

The third area of experience is derived from working for a federal government or state agency. For example, a person with many years of experience as an investigator in the Division of Enforcement at the SEC could bring helpful testimony to a securities industry matter. A research analyst in the Division of Economics at the CFTC could well provide expert testimony involving a "hedge-to-arrive" agreement that went bad.

There is a word of caution for those who have developed a career path with a federal or state government agency. Clearly, expert witnesses who have vast government work experience are most often viewed quite favorably by the public. However, some members of a jury, and some judges too for that matter, suspect that long periods of time spent with a regulatory agency may well bring a certain built-in bias to the expert's testimony. To be effective, the expert with strong government experience must develop her testimony style with extra care to ensure that her delivery comes across as being well balanced, thoughtful and credible.

For qualification purposes a person who has a combination of industry, academia and regulatory work experience would certainly seem to be the most attractive candidate for expert witness work. Any combination of two of the three backgrounds would clearly provide the second best set of credentials for an expert witness. If only one of the three experiences were to prevail, successful industry experience would seem to be the preferred in most instances.

Whatever experience you bring to the litigation table, make sure you package it carefully. Expert witnesses must present their background to the court with dignity and professionalism. Under no circumstances should you let the work experience of your opposing expert erode your poise and confidence. Even if the other expert has far more experience than you, chances are you have special qualities that he doesn't posses. It is critical you identify that "special something" early on and capitalize on it in your testimony. This will help the judge, jury, or arbitration panel arrive at a sound decision.

Chapter V

Marketing Your Credentials

Do what you can, with what you have, where you are.
                                        -Theodore Roosevelt

There is an old adage that says *you can't judge a book by its cover*. While that may well be true, there is a second, and perhaps more powerful and accurate proverb which says, *first impressions are lasting impressions*. The images we portray to others are lasting and have three components. They are: appearance, personality and intelligence.

In terms of our physical appearance, we must accept the fact that we are who we are. It has been said that nearly seventy-five percent of all people are in some way not pleased with the way they look. People all too often view themselves as being either too tall or too short. Others look at themselves as being too slender or overweight. Many people do not find their facial features attractive.

Aside from being able to lose weight or seek the assistance of a qualified cosmetic surgeon to make certain facial modifications to our looks, for the most part, we really can't change much of our basic physical make-up. But there are some things you can do that, when done successfully, will have a powerful impact on your success as an expert witness.

It is critical you appear well groomed at all times. You want to "Dress for Success."

For men, that generally means being clean shaven. For both women and men, they should maintain a professional hair style. This suggestion may seem a bit old fashioned, but there is a good chance that many jury members will be a bit old fashioned themselves. After all, it is the jury you will be appealing to at trial. It is equally important to try to portray a 'healthy' look, regardless of age.

The *Power* of Appearance

Ultimately, a person's dress code will say it all. Your attire represents who you are. It becomes your image and sets the stage as to how others will perceive you. Your appearance will often speak volumes as to what you stand for. Your physical appearance forms lasting impressions. Your 'dress' becomes symbolic of your persona.

An expert witness wardrobe will generally include a dark, or pinstripe suit (blue, gray, brown or charcoal). Each color projects an image of you in time and place. It sends a specific message to others who will be observing you. For example, dark blue is a symbolic color of authority or power. Gray has intellectual overtones. It is a cerebral color associated often with academia. Brown on the other hand is the color of warmth or friendliness. "Teddy Bear" brown suggests, "I want to be your friend." Charcoal is an "ending" color. It is best worn at the closing of the proceeding.

For example, when appearing for deposition, (for men) wearing a dark blue, pinstripe suit with white shirt and a dark red tie with a simple print or logo and (for women) a dark suit with white blouse and a dark red print scarf, sends the message to the opposing side that they are here to do serious business. You want to set the tone that the deposition will be conducted professionally, or you will not participate. You want to send the message unequivocally, that although it is his deposition, you are the one who truly is in control. You want to set the tone that you are a powerful force to be reckoned with and that the deposition process must be kept on a high level. One thing you want to make clear from the outset and that is under no circumstances will you tolerate any *ad hominem* attacks.

A number of people do not have a charming personality.

During the trial, especially a jury trial, you want to send a friendly message to the judge and jury. The first day of trial you give direct testimony. This is friendly territory. It is a day of introductions. Remember, you want to be liked by the jury, but most important you want to be trusted. This is the day your credentials are presented and examined for qualification to testify before the court. Always be aware that first impressions are lasting impressions. Also, if you are testifying before an arbitration panel, be sure to ask instructing counsel what dress code the arbitrators have adopted. It is always appropriate to follow their lead – which may, in some instances, be more casual than you would expect. If in doubt, err on the side of caution and formality.

Should there be a second day of testimony you might choose to wear a gray suit. Establish yourself as the teacher. Your presentation must be didactic. You bring to the table a vast amount of knowledge and experience to share with the jury in helping them arrive at the right decision. For both women and men, do try and stay with solid white blouses and shirts, as white is a formal color, and the courtroom atmosphere is formal.

On the first day of cross-examination, you can accurately predict the dress code for the day, right? Dark blue, pinstripe suit with white shirt and dark red tie with a modest design. This is the same uniform you wore on the first day of your deposition. You want to remind opposing counsel who really is in command of the testimony. You want to insist that counsel keep cross-examination on a professional level at all times.

Finally, on re-direct, if the hearing schedule permits, a solid charcoal suit with white shirt and, for men a corresponding print tie may be appropriate. This phase of the trial is bringing closure to your testimony. You want to leave the judge and jury with a warm image. You want to leave a lasting impression in their minds that your testimony had authority and conviction over the facts in the case.

Your dress should always be conventional, not fashionable. You should avoid the latest fashion and stay with a conservative look, tried and tested. There are a number of acceptable labels out there which offer a modest price line of formal dress wear for both women and men. Of course, one can never go wrong with Brooks Brothers. In his text, *Generations of Style,* fashion designer John William Cooke quotes Winthrop H. Brooks, President of Brooks Brothers (1935-1946) as saying:

> *"And right here let me say a word about conservatism. It does not mean, as so many believe or affect to believe, a stubborn refusal to discard what is old and outworn, nor an old fogeyish prejudice against innovations of any kind. It really means a determination to retain what has been tried and proven to be good, and to refrain from the exploitation,*

simply because it is new, of what is essentially cheap and silly."[38]

The company has stores in most major cities in the United States. The firm's attire has stood the test of time.

Let Your Experience Speak

Your intellect is what it is. Perhaps you have formal education that has prepared you well to be a litigation consultant and expert witness. On the other hand, you may have achieved a wealth of knowledge through hands-on work experience to do the task. Perhaps you have a combination of the two, formal education and training, which brings a dynamic set of credentials which the jury can rely upon in assisting them in reaching their final conclusions in the matter before the court.

Either way, it is important that you do two things. First, you need to remain current in your field. This means you must attend seminars and conferences regularly. You should read books and publications which will help you to keep abreast of changes and happenings in your particular industry and field of expertise. Second, and most important, you must be able to: 1) mobilize your knowledge and experience, 2) analyze the facts in the case and 3) ultimately articulate your views to the judge and jury effectively.

You possess an extraordinary set of experiences comprised of industry hands-on work. You have "attained the sum of wisdom."[39] You have had a brief stint in related government work and teach part-time in your field of expertise at a local college. You have a solid command of the English language. When you speak, people listen. You look and dress the part; you have all the qualifications to be a successful litigation consultant. You would make an excellent expert witness in every way. In other words, you have all the ingredients to be triumphant as a litigation consultant and expert witness. There is just one problem: no top drawer trial lawyers know you exist.

In order to be successful and prosper as an expert witness, you have got to get yourself known. Remember this, the more trial lawyers who know you exist; the more litigation work will be likely to come your way.

38   Cooke, John William. *Generations of Style*. New York: Brooks Brothers, Inc., 2003, p. 7.
39   Milton, John. *Paradise Lost*. Mineola: Dover Publications, Inc., 2005, p. 260.

The curriculum vitae is the most effective marketing tool experts use to introduce themselves to the trial lawyer community. That document has to be powerful. The CV must capture the imagination of the reader instantly and cause her to contact you immediately. The preparation of this document is discussed thoroughly in Chapter VII and a sample CV is made available for ready reference in Appendix B.

Once your appearance is in check and your CV is compiled properly, you are ready to engage into the full marketing phase. The first step is to identify those law firms that have a legal expertise compatible with your area of specialty. For example, if your field is securities, you would certainly want to make the acquaintance of Wall Street law firms catering to the stock brokerage community. You would also want to be well known at the SEC. To avoid any possible conflicts of interest, Federal regulatory agencies typically do not make specific referrals of consultants and expert witnesses to law firms. When asked, however, they will often provide three or four names of litigation consultants familiar to them to the party making the inquiry. From that listing, law firms have a set of recognizable names from which they can conduct their own independent search and make an ultimate selection. You certainly want to have your name on such a list.

Law firms can be divided into four categories. There are large, multi-capable firms which have at their disposal an abundance of resources to handle nearly any type of case that may be brought to their doorstep. There are *specialty* or *boutique* firms. These law firms have developed a specific legal expertise within a given industry. Examples of such firms might be antitrust law firms and firms that specialize in medical malpractice suits. The third category of law firm is the medium-sized firm. These are firms which, for the most part, have a broad, well-diversified practice. They have a sizeable legal team on board, are located in medium-sized cities across the United States and tend to have a regional focus in the services they provide to the public. The fourth category of law practice is the sole practitioner. These legal entrepreneurs reside in cities, towns and villages throughout the United States. These lawyers may specialize in a particular field or handle a variety of cases. For the most part, they are multi-task attorneys who provide a number of legal services to members of the community in which they live. For the most part, this describes the legal community within America.

When developing a marketing plan, use the "rifle approach." It is the most effective strategy in a marketing schematic. What I mean by the "rifle approach" as opposed to the "shotgun" approach is this. Rather than scattering your marketing effort among a target audience which includes a large number of law firms with an expanded legal practice, use the rifle approach. Zero in on a handful of law firms whose practice is strategically compatible with your particular field of expertise. This saves you both time and money in developing an efficient marketing program.

Second, expand your marketing effort to include those large and multi-task law firms. Arrange to meet their staff in person. One way this can be accomplished is by attending legal conferences. Another way is to invite lawyers to breakfast or lunch. Face-to-face contact goes a long way in developing meaningful and lasting relationships.

A Houston-based refining and marketing company became the target of a federal government lawsuit. The oil company retained a local law firm to defend them in the matter. I was referred to that law firm as a possible candidate to be included on the firm's litigation team. As a part of the "vetting" process, the lead trial lawyer in the case flew to Pennsylvania and arranged to interview me at my home. He later engaged me to be a part of his team. The case went to a jury trial. A verdict later came down in favor of the defendant. The lawyer had gone to great lengths to build a first-rate litigation team and his efforts had clearly paid off.[40]

I suggest you let the medium-sized firms and the sole practitioners seek you out. You have precious time and limited resources to market your credentials. Therefore, the carefully aimed approach to marketing, as opposed to the "shotgun" approach, will typically be the most effective and cost beneficial in the long run.

Your marketing plan should include direct mailers to both lawyers and regulatory agencies. Participate in speaking engagements before Bar Association conferences. Write journal articles. Serve as an arbitrator on arbitration panels. Use association membership listings and legal directories to develop your prospect mailing list. Of course, the internet is a valuable tool to make your availability known. Finally, develop and

---

40   Appendix G.

maintain an active website and have your site readily available on the major search engines such as Google and Yahoo.

Once you have been asked to do litigation consultant or expert witness work, do stay in touch with the trial lawyers who hired you. They are a tremendous resource to draw upon for referrals.

One of the best ways to stay in touch with lawyers, who have hired you to do litigation work in the past, is to send holiday cards to them annually. It is an economical and thoughtful way to keep your name current on their radar screens.

A telephone call now and then to old lawyer friends will go a long way. While they may not have an engagement for you right now, they may know a lawyer who is looking for litigation assistance and refer you to that person. Remember lawyers have corporate clients and while your field of expertise may not be needed as a litigation consultant or expert witness, the corporate client firm may well be in need of your expertise as a consultant on other matters related to their general business operation.

To illustrate, some years ago I was asked to represent the president of an energy refining and marketing company in a litigation matter. After that case had been concluded, the president asked me to assist his firm in developing a comprehensive set of internal controls in the form of a written policy and procedures manual. The goal was to have in place a written set of guidelines for employees to follow. The objective was to limit any litigation exposure in the future. That litigation assignment was followed by ten years of management consultant assignments.

In this business of litigation support and expert witness work, one never knows when the telephone will ring with a new project opportunity on the horizon. But one thing is certain: by managing actively an aggressive marketing program, you increase your chances of having the telephone ringing more often than the person who sits idle and doesn't market his credentials at all.

Chapter VI

Compensation

> *It is not the employer who pays wages-he only handles the money. It is the product that pays wages.*
>
> -Henry Ford

The most common questions asked by the new litigation consultant is, "What do I charge and how do I get paid for my services?"

Your *services* are your *product*.

Your services are derived from your intellectual property. They are listed in your *Curriculum Vitae*. Your services are eventually revealed in the form of a carefully prepared and professionally written *Expert Report*. These components have value and payment is derived from an industry fee schedule. A problem that many litigation consultants and expert witnesses have is keeping current with their prevailing industry's consultant fee schedule.

In general, litigation consultant work is billed at an hourly rate. Work begins with a review of the complaint and the respondent's answer to that complaint. An examination of pertinent documents associated with the case usually comes next. Thereafter analysis is performed and exhibits are prepared. This ends with the preparation of a professionally written Expert Report. Most experts charge for their work based on an hourly rate. Other experts charge a flat fee per day, or daily rate.

Litigation consultant and expert testimony fee schedules are in large part governed by each industry grouping being represented. Within that general industry framework, consultants and experts should charge fees based on their particular qualifications and previous experience as an expert witness. The demands of the various tasks which need to be accomplished in case formulation will also impact the contemplated fee structure.

Because of its scientific and technological nature, the **medical** industry has a tendency to capture the high end of the fee schedule for expert witness testimony. Experts may be required to have a background in biology. Other experts may be required to have skills in computer science applications involving forensic tests or medical techniques. To be qualified as an expert in a particular field, the litigation consultant may be required to have heightened academic credentials, or advanced degrees in their respective fields of study such as computer science, natural science or medicine.

Experts in the field of **medicine** command billing rates in the range of $1,000 to $1,500 an hour. In certain circumstances, a daily fee of $10,000 would not be unusual. An example of a high profile case which could give rise to such fees for criminologists and forensic experts is the horrific 2009 murder of Yale graduate student Annie Le.

For those experts who plan on providing litigation support work for the **construction** industry, the consultant will often need academic credentials involving various parts of engineering as well as in-depth work experience. In these instances, an hourly fee structure in the range of $350 to $450 an hour would seem to be quite acceptable. A daily fee of $3,500 is reasonable.

The **securities** and **futures** industries in many respects mirror the medical industry in establishing a fee schedule. Case diversity and complexity drive the fee structure. Some parts of securities and futures cases may require an expert with a legal background. In other words, a matter may require a person to have a law degree. Other cases may require a person who has done advanced academic work in the field of economics.

Clearly, anyone who is considering providing litigation consultant and expert witness work involving swap and derivative instruments must have an academic background focused in finance and mathematics. The complexity of the nature of these products, their pricing schematic and impact on financial market systems requires experts who are well versed in these academic disciplines. Other cases may require in-depth general industry or regulatory experience. Again, depending on the case, hourly billing rates may range from $750 to $1,000 an hour. A daily fee of $10,000 may not be unusual.

Although the party you are representing is ultimately responsible for the payment of your consultant services in the matter, never contract directly with that person or their entity (business). You should only contract with the law firm representing the plaintiff or defendant, as the case may be. Obtain a letter of engagement from the law firm, signed by the trial lawyer assigned to the case as well as a retainer fee. These materials should be received before you commence work. Recall earlier, this retainer and payment procedure is important especially when the engagement involves a criminal matter.

I have always suggested to the trial lawyers who have asked me to do litigation consultant work that the litigation assignment be done in phases. In addition, I have asked that each phase be funded independently prior to work commencing on each particular phase. By structuring the case development this way, the law firm's client can better plan financially for each phase of the project and at the same time actually see the case unfold. This approach includes the client in the process and is more likely to gain the client's overall support during the case formulation phase. That is to say, if the trial lawyer is able to show his client your work as it passes through the various stages of development, then the client is more apt to budget enthusiastically for the next phase with positive support for your continued involvement.

This process is important for a number of reasons. First, the most expensive phase of the litigation consultant's involvement is the development of her Expert Report. This document is her testimony at deposition and trial. The expert's ultimate success or failure rests on the quality of this product. The Expert Report must be a document of perfection. To achieve that goal, the preparation and completion of the expert report will require adequate funding. If you fail to get that full commitment upfront, pass on the assignment. Always keep in mind that your professional reputation is at stake.

In closing, there are a couple of items I would like to add regarding compensation schedules and getting paid. Fee schedules do not include production costs of materials, technological support for exhibit preparation and development. Travel and lodging expenses will of course be required to visit the law firm making representation as well as travel to have your deposition taken and trial testimony. Those items must be funded independently of your hourly or daily work fee schedule. These issues must be clearly addressed in the lawyer's engagement letter to you.

Chapter VII

Curriculum Vitae

> *Letters of social reference are never baldly requested by anyone, and the wise friend never gives one except obliquely.*
>
> —Amy Vanderbilt[41]

Metaphorically, the Curriculum Vitae (CV) is a "letter of reference." It is used to introduce you personally, and your professional credentials to the legal community.

Your *CV* is the most effective tool in your marketing toolbox.

It is also an official document which presents your credentials to a court or arbitration panel and will be used to certify that you are qualified to testify as an expert witness before the court or hearing panel. Your CV is a document which can be used against you at a deposition hearing. If your CV is deficient, or perceived to be lacking in any way, opposing counsel will use that document against you. First, he will attempt to have you disqualified as an expert for failing to have disclosed fully some part of your background. If that fails, he will begin to engage in *ad hominem* attacks and character assassination.

Nancy Cavender is Professor Emeritus at the College of Marin. In her text, *Logic and Contemporary Rhetoric*, she argues that "Although attacks on a person usually are irrelevant to that individual's argument or claims, sometimes they are relevant indeed."[42] She continues by saying:

> **"Lawyers who attack the testimony of courtroom witnesses by questioning their expertise or character are not**

---

41 Vanderbilt, Amy. *Amy Vanderbilt's Etiquette.* Garden City: Doubleday & Company, 1972, p. 537.

42 Cavender, Nancy M. and Kahane, Howard. *Logic and Contemporary Rhetoric.* Belmont: Wadsworth CENGAGE Learning, 2010, p. 74.

necessarily guilty of arguing ad hominem. *They may be trying to gauge the integrity of the witness to determine whether his or her testimony is credible."*[43]

Your CV must be accurate and complete.

You do not want to run the risk of having opposing counsel begin a line of questioning which aims to undermine your integrity and thereby gives cause for questioning the credibility of your testimony. A complete and accurate presentation of your credentials in your CV will prevent this from happening. The information you impart in your CV must at a minimum include: 1) your name, 2) address and 3) telecommunication contact methods. The CV must describe in detail your work experience and educational background. It should also include supplemental information which you feel your audience, namely the court and the jury, might find pertinent or perhaps impressive. Find something that might make you standout from others. For example, if you were awarded the Medal of Freedom or the (Congressional) Medal of Honor by the President, that certainly would be something that makes you special.

You may wish to include certain attachments to your CV. For example, if you have participated in a number of speaking engagements before related industry groups or lectured in an academic setting, list them. This demonstrates to the engaging law firm that you have the ability and confidence to speak before people (i.e., a jury) and not get stage fright. If you have written journal articles or published a book on the topic which you intend to testify on, list them too. All activities which make you special - that is value added to the court - include them in your CV.

If you have experience testifying as an expert witness in the past, it is important you make a listing of those appearances. In fact, courts require you to disclose all cases in which you have given testimony, either in deposition or court, in the previous four years. I prefer to include my litigation experience separately from the CV, but I do make it available in the same marketing package when I am making an initial contact with a law firm that is interested in engaging me to do litigation consultant work. At a minimum, your litigation listing should include the case caption with the court-assigned docket number, the

---

43   Ibid.

venue, whether you represented the plaintiff or the defendant, and the outcome. In other words, was the verdict favorable or unfavorable to the side you were representing? Ideally, your litigation case listing will reveal work done equally balanced between claimant (plaintiff) and respondent (defendant) engagements. This sends a strong message to the court that your work is reliable and unbiased.

How to Construct your *CV*:

FRONT COVER PAGE

This first page of your CV should include: 1) your name, 2) full address and 3) points of contact. Points of contact are your: 1) home and business telephone numbers, 2) cell telephone number and 3) e-mail address. Make sure all telephone numbers have a message system to ensure you don't miss a potential business call. The world is becoming increasingly flat.

Litigation support assignments may well include locations outside the United States. If you are fluent in a language other than English, you should put that information up front. Finally, if you hold, or have held licenses in the industry you are holding yourself out as a specialist, include them too, on the cover page.

This might consist of: 1) securities registrations, 2) real estate licenses or 3) medical licenses and certifications. In other words, anything that makes you special - something that makes you standout from others - include that information on the front cover page of your CV.

PROFESSIONAL EXPERIENCE

The second page of your CV should begin with a detailed summary of your *work experience*. Here you tell of your career and accomplishments. Include job title and location of your work station. For example, if you were an Assistant Manager of your firm's plant location in Flint, Michigan note Flint, Michigan beneath your position. Don't forget to include dates associated with your work station entry. Later, if you were promoted to Plant Manager of the Pittsburgh plant, make a separate entry to note that fact, even though the employment was with the same company. The *professional experience* section of your CV must describe a successful career. It should represent your promotions and related job title enhancements.

PROFESSIONAL DEVELOPMENT

Most organizations are desirous that their executives keep current with industry changes and newly-devised management techniques. These *Executive Training Programs* are sponsored by some of the finest colleges and universities in the nation. It is important you list them. This evidences you keep abreast of what's going on in your industry. Upon completion of training, these institutions of higher learning award each participant with a formal certificate of training. It is important that this training be archived in a section separate from your formal education. You don't want to run the risk of being accused of holding yourself out as having a degree from a college or university where that is not the case.

MILITARY EXPERIENCE

Military experience is important. There is a strong chance that at least one jury member will have served time in the United States armed forces. Many members of the jury are patriots. Your military service will go a long way in portraying your true character. The entries on your CV should include: 1) branch of service, 2) initial date of entry into military service, 3) date of discharge or retirement and 4) your testament to your *Honorable* discharge. You should include your rank upon entry into the military and your ending rank upon separation from service.

EDUCATION

The following section on your CV should be a listing of your formal *Education*. It should begin with the highest degree earned and in what field. This information should be followed with the name and address of the college or university from which you earned your degree. Dates of attendance are mandatory. Postgraduate work should be included in this section with the appropriate notations.

PUBLICATIONS

This section of your CV is very important. This section not only demonstrates your ongoing professional involvement in your career industry, but also evidences you are recognized as an expert in your field. These disclosures provide the judge supporting evidence to declare you an expert in the case before his court. This section should begin by listing any *books* you have authored. The next listing should include any *journal articles* you have written.

CONFERENCE PROCEEDINGS

All industry-related *conferences* you have attended and participated in as a panelist or conference speaker should be listed. The date and location, as well as the title of the conference, should be listed.

NEWSPAPERS AND PERIODICALS

A listing of all articles you have written for *magazines* and *newspapers* should be a part of your CV. The title of the column, the name of the magazine or newspaper and the date the article appeared should be included in the listing. Kate L. Turabian (1893-1987) was an American educator. Her text, *A Manual for Writers of Term Papers, Theses, and Dissertations* has provided grammar and structural guidance to writers since 1937.[44]

AWARDS

The last section of your CV should list formal *Awards* you have received in recognition of exemplary work in your career field. Listings may also include civic awards as well. For example, should you be awarded your community's award for some special civic project you were involved in, that too, should be included. Military awards however, I would include in the military section of your CV, and not here. A *Sample Curriculum Vitae* is included on page 90 of the Appendix.[45]

Is the CV complete?

The question often arises, what makes a CV complete? How far back in time must one go in listing academic and work history to satisfy this requirement? At first blush, ten years of work experience and a posting of a person's highest academic degree would seem to be reasonable. Based on hardened experience, I recommend that expert witnesses list their entire work history. The work history listing should be in ascending order. That means, the most current work position would be at the top of the page and the first job the expert had, would be at the bottom of the page(s). The first job listing should reflect a person's employment

---

[44] Turabian, Kate L. *A Manual for Writers of Term Papers, Theses, and Dissertations.* Chicago: The University of Chicago Press, 1996.

[45] Appendix B.

after completion of military service or college graduation, whichever is applicable. I further recommend that if a person has attended more than one college during their formal education experience, list all colleges and universities attended with dates of attendance. For example, if an expert witness graduated from the Pennsylvania State University, but attended a community college his first two years of formal education, list both colleges on the CV and not just Penn State. In the *Tales from the Hot Seat* chapter, I include amusing stories which will lend support for this recommendation.

To ensure your CV will be accepted by the court or arbitration hearing panel, I suggest you compile a list of documents which will support each entry you have made on your CV. That is to say:

You must develop a *Curriculum Vitae Certification Binder*.

If properly constructed, this tool will provide you with sufficient ammunition to deflect effectively any attempt by opposing counsel who is desirous of engaging in character assassination on your person and destruction of your contemplated testimony.

Curriculum Vitae Certification Binder

Your CV Certification Binder should mirror your CV in construction methodology. Specifically, in section one of your Certification Binder you should archive supporting documents of your listing on page one of your CV. For example, in this section of your CV Certification Binder you should include any foreign language certificates of completion you have received. Copies of formal registrations and licenses should be archived in this section of your Certification Binder as well. Your work experience section should include copies of work engagement letters or contracts. There should be some document that evidences you work where you say you work and that you hold the position and title you say you do.

Your professional development section should at a minimum, have a copy of your training certificate of completion. If you are able to retain a curriculum listing of what the course was about, that may well be helpful to have on hand. Opposing counsel may ask you about that training. If the training was 30 years ago, as was the situation in my case, to have a copy of the course agenda will be handy in jogging your memory.

Your military section should include copies of your discharge and copies of any military awards you may have received while serving in the armed forces. Copies of letters of recognition and assignment would be good to have available. The education section of your CV Certification Binder should contain copies of your college or university degrees. Should you have been awarded any academic achievement awards, such as Phi Beta Kappa, include copies of those documents as well.

The publications, conferences, newspapers and periodicals sections, all should contain copies of at least the front page of those pertinent documents. If you have written books, a copy of the dust jacket will be sufficient. Copies of program handouts, curriculum and other materials associated with these activities should be retained and become a part of your CV Certification Binder.

The last section of your CV Certification Binder is the awards section. Here, include copies of the awards you have received. If the award is a plaque, photocopy the plaque, and make that a part of your CV Certification Binder.

Chapter VIII

Engagement Letter

> *A verbal contract isn't worth the paper it's written on.*
>
> -Samuel Goldwyn

The Engagement Letter you receive from the retaining law firm should clearly explain what is expected of you as a litigation consultant in the matter and should the case go to trial, what is expected of you as an expert witness. I have always recommended to trial lawyers seeking my litigation support services to scope my work in phases. I have further suggested that each phase be funded independently one from the other. By doing so, both the law firm and the client being represented can better plan for the funding of each phase of the litigation support project. Here, the client is more fully engaged in the litigation process and can actually see the case work unfold. That is to say, if the client is able to see the work product develop as it passes through each phase, the client will be more apt to budget enthusiastically for the next phase.

Your role as a litigation consultant or non-testifying expert may transition to that of an expert witness, or testifying expert. If that happens, be sure to commence a new and clearly defined Engagement Letter with retaining counsel. This phase of the litigation process will take on a new dimension. For example, all communication with instructing counsel during the consulting stage is clearly identifiable as such for the purpose of privilege and "work product" protection. Once you are designated as a testifying expert, care should be taken to ensure that the litigation team understands what documents and communication may have to be produced to the other side during discovery.

The *Engagement Letter* is a legal document which authorizes you to conduct work in a case, receive payment for your services and ensure protection of your work product.

The Engagement Letter should begin with an explanation as to the essence of the assignment. The next section of that document must clearly outline your fee schedule and the manner in which you will get paid. Finally, the Engagement Letter should articulate clearly any prohibited activities and address all aspects of *confidentiality*.

Work Product Immunity

> *"FRCP Rule 26 (b) (3) provides* **limited protection** *to otherwise discoverable trial preparation and work product materials. Such materials are subject to discovery only when the information is not* **reasonably** *available from any other source, and when the discovering party has* **substantial** *need for information. The work product protection applies only to* **documents** *prepared by or on behalf of an attorney in anticipation of litigation. On the other hand, the mental impressions and the legal evaluations of an attorney, investigator, or claims agent enjoy* **absolute privilege** *from disclosure."*[46]

Experts

> *"Parties are generally allowed to depose an opposing party's expert witnesses who are expected to* **testify** *at trial. Only in certain* **exceptional circumstances** *are opposing parties allowed to obtain discovery relating to experts not expected to testify at trial. No discovery is allowed with respect to any expert that is merely* **consulted** *but not retained."*[47]

---

46 Concepcion, Natasha. *Civil Procedure*. New York: Barnes & Noble Publishing, 2003, pp. 3-4.
47 Ibid, p. 4.

With respect to the Confidentiality section of the Engagement Letter, it must be made clear with no equivocation, that unless ordered by a court, under no circumstances can the engaging law firm make any part of your work product available to a third party. Your work product is proprietary in nature. Your work product is your intellectual property. Should any of that work be disclosed to a third party, you run the risk of compromising work to be done in future cases. Never allow this to happen. If this should take place, you should report this development immediately to your personal attorney and the bar association of the state involved.

The Engagement Letter should address the manner in which materials will be provided to you to prepare the Expert Report, and the manner in which they should be returned to the engaging law firm. There should be a Termination clause in your Engagement Letter as well as a Closing Matters or Miscellaneous paragraph at the end of the document. Finally, the Engagement Letter should end with signature blocks and dates of execution - one each for the lawyer to sign and a place for your signature indicating acceptance of the terms. The original letter should be returned to the lawyer and you should retain a copy in your files. A *Sample Engagement Letter* is in the Appendices and can be found on page 93 of the text.[48]

---

48   Appendix C.

Chapter IX

Expert Report

The world is governed by opinion.
                                        -Thomas Hobbes

The most important phase of the litigation consultant's work schedule is the development and completion of the Expert Report. This document provides the foundation for your testimony at deposition and trial. Your success or failure as an expert witness rests on the quality of this report. The Expert Report must pass the test of perfection.

Case formulation begins with the reading of the complaint and the respondent's answer. Other important materials for review include: 1) deposition transcripts of the various parties involved with the case, 2) motions, 3) stipulations and 4) other pertinent information.

There are three basic methods which an expert witness may be asked by counsel to use in providing testimony in a lawsuit. They are: 1) affidavit, 2) declaration and 3) expert report. An *affidavit* is a written statement confirmed by oath or affirmation for use as evidence in court. A *declaration* is an affirmation made instead of taking an oath, usually in writing. The *expert report* on the other hand, is a comprehensive written document comprised of three information groupings: 1) the expert's professional background, or work experience and education, 2) a chronological history of the case formulation process and 3) the expert's findings, opinions and conclusions in the matter.

Keep in mind the Expert Report does not include what is commonly referred to as your "work product." (See the Glossary of Terms: Expert Report and Work Product). Because people operate in a world of symbols, always include in your expert report: 1) a bibliography listing all source documents relied upon to develop the narrative, 2) tables,

3) charts and 4) graphs. A *Sample Expert Report* is provided on page 97 in the Appendix.[49]

The *Expert Report* provides the foundation for your oral testimony at *deposition* and *trial*.

It is critical, that your Expert Report be written to perfection. Some years ago, I was asked by a boutique law firm based in New York to assist it in a litigation matter. The assignment was to serve as a litigation consultant and later provide testimony as an expert witness should the case go to trial - which it did. The matter was very complicated and involved a number of issues concerning the trading of certain futures contracts on the Commodity Exchange, Inc. (COMEX). The law firm that retained me represented the defendant in the matter.

The Expert Report I prepared in that case was one of the most comprehensive documents in my twenty-three years as a litigation consultant and expert witness. I thought it would be helpful to recreate here the steps I went through in that action leading up to and including the preparation of the Expert Report.

The first step leading to the construction of my Expert Report was to identify the persons, business relationships and related activities involved in the matter. The second step was to identify those parties whose business lines may have required some form of state licensing or registration with Federal authorities. This is most important because parties whose businesses require regulatory oversight are required to abide by a specific set of regulatory rules and regulations. If they fail to do so, they may be operating outside the law. If found guilty, the parties involved can: 1) be fined, 2) lose their license or registration, 3) be barred from the industry permanently, or perhaps, 4) be sent to prison.

The third step which I did in the case and what you must do is to review and catalog all pertinent documents which will be used to prepare the Expert Report. A listing of those documents should be made and included as an Appendix to the Expert Report. Only documents used to prepare the Expert Report should be on that listing. Only documents on the listing may be referred to when giving deposition or trial testimony. Examples of documents used to prepare an Expert Report include items such as: 1) account documents, 2) applications, 3) employment agreements, 4) contracts of initial engagement, 5) policy

---

49   Appendix D.

statements, 6) employee handbooks, 7) policy and procedure manuals, 8) internal and external audit reports, 9) affidavits and declarations from interested parties, and 10) deposition transcripts of testimony taken of parties connected with the case.

This information will enable you to start developing each section of your report. Those sections should be clearly marked, either by numbering or perhaps bold type letters. Each section should have a heading to make for easy reference. You want to make certain your testimony themes: 1) flow, 2) are well articulated and 3) earmark critical elements in your case and are highlighted. Keep in mind, your goal is to corroborate each and every point you desire to make in either support of or rebuttal to, a particular allegation in the complaint.

At this stage, you should begin framing your testimony. A good way to start is by developing an outline of your contemplated presentation. Most of my Expert Reports, and the one I am referencing here, follow a similar format. In general, the sections are presented in this fashion: 1) a cover page which lists; a) your name, b) the caption of the lawsuit and c) the date of your report, 2) qualifications, 3) scope of engagement, 4) materials consulted and relied upon in reaching opinions and conclusions, 5) summary of findings, 6) summary of opinions and conclusions, 7) overview of events, 8) background, 9) analysis, 10) findings and opinions and 11) conclusion.[50]

A word of caution in developing your Expert Report and later giving oral testimony is appropriate. If your case involves matters governed by federal regulations do not identify any specific activity as being violative of those regulations. That is the fact-finder's job, and many courts will take offense to such notation by experts. You may, on the other hand, cite standard customs, practices and usages of the industry and note a departure of those practices in your report. You can also note industry standards or practices relative to your case, and a departure or potential violation of those industry rules in your report. You can cite breach of company policy, or operating outside of company policy and procedures. All of this is perfectly acceptable - just stay away from appearing to do the hearing panel's job or the work of the judge assigned to the case.

---

50   Ibid

Chapter X

Peer Review

> *It is not best that we should all think alike; it is difference of opinion which makes horse races.*
> —Mark Twain

One of the first questions you may be asked at deposition by opposing counsel is, "Has your work product been peer reviewed?" A negative response puts you immediately on the defensive and this is not the way you want your testimony to begin.

What is peer review? How does it work? Who would be a peer you could draw upon to review your Expert Report? Why is it necessary that you have your report peer reviewed?

Assume that an expert witness in a case happens to be a medical doctor who specializes in pediatrics. A peer review of her work would best be done by another medical doctor who specializes in the medical care of children. An expert witness who is a computer scientist specializing in browsers would be best served to have his work reviewed by a computer scientist with a similar background. A mechanical engineer who plans to testify in a case as an expert witness should have her work product reviewed by a person with like credentials. That is to say, the person you select to make a peer review of your Expert Report should have similar work experience which is a mirror image of your professional credentials.

Typically, the person making a peer review of your Expert Report will provide a written report of findings based on her review of your work product. This procedure gives credibility to the process and provides a heightened degree of confidence as to the relevancy and reliability of the information stated in your Expert Report.

There are times when a third-party review is required. This occurs when part of your testimony includes information or analysis which is beyond your scope or primary field of expertise. For example, assume a medical doctor plans to give testimony that will include an opinion on certain medication which had been prescribed to treat a patient for a specific illness or condition, and that patient is now a claimant in a litigation case. The medical doctor may seek the services of a third party such as a pharmacologist, who would explain the compounds which make up the drug used for treatment. She might further provide information about the drug such as: 1) what age group is it typically prescribed, 2) for what illness is it usually effective, 3) how the drug works in the patient's system and 4) what negative consequences might arise from treatment.

As in the case of peer review, this procedure adds credibility and confidence to the litigation process. It provides the trier(s) of fact a degree of comfort "... that an expert's testimony both rests on a reliable foundation and is relevant to the task at hand."[51]

The process of obtaining peer or third-party review can be time consuming and most challenging. Once a candidate for peer review is identified, you must proffer that candidate's name to the lawyer who initially engaged you in the case. That lawyer will in turn contact your peer or third-party reviewer in order to arrange for an interview and make examination of that person's credentials to ensure they are qualified to act as your peer reviewer in the matter. If found qualified, the lawyer will scope the peer review engagement and specify the requirements for the review and the expected analysis to be performed. A fee schedule and budget will be established between the lawyer and the peer reviewer. Once all parties are in agreement, counsel will contract with the peer reviewer directly and execute a formal engagement letter to have the peer review task conducted.

Among other things, the peer or third-party review will include an analysis of the data you relied upon to make findings and draw conclusions as stated in your Expert Report. The peer or third-party reviewer should opine on the methods and applications used in constructing your Expert Report, and make some reference that those

---

51   Grady, Allison. *Daubert* and Expert Testimony. *Virtual Mentor.* February 2006, Volume 8, Number 2: 97-100, pp. 1-2.

methodologies are standard customs, practices and usages within the industry you both represent. The reviewer should include the outcomes of measurable test results in the opinions and conclusions section of the report. The peer or third-party review findings are memorialized in the form of a written report, typically a sworn affidavit, and are provided directly to the engaging law firm. You should not be privy to the contents of that report until the trial is concluded. Then, and only then, should the engaging lawyer provide you a copy of your peer reviewer's report. This ensures integrity of the peer review process.

At a minimum, the peer or third-party reviewer's sworn affidavit should include: 1) a statement of that person's professional credentials to include educational background, 2) a statement as to the applicable parts of your Expert Report the reviewer was asked to make findings and render an opinion on, and 3) in the conclusion section of the reviewer's report, there should be a clear statement as to whether or not there was a concurrence or non-concurrence with the general contents and conclusion in your Expert Report. If there is a non-concurrence, the reviewer's report should clearly state why such non-concurrence exists. Finally, in the conclusion section of the reviewer's report, there needs to be a summary statement which describes fully the reviewer's independent analysis of your report. The reviewer's CV will be attached to her affidavit. This package of materials should then be sent directly from the reviewer to the engaging law firm. As noted earlier, it is important you not see this report prior to submission.

There is legal precedence for having your litigation work product peer reviewed. On June 28, 1993, Supreme Court Justice Harry Blackmun delivered the opinion for a unanimous Court in *William Daubert, et ux, etc., et al., Petitioners vs. Merrill Dow Pharmaceuticals, Inc.*, and in doing so, noted "…the Court offered 4 concrete questions to be kept in mind when determining the reliability of expert testimony [12]."

- Can the idea or theory be tested via the scientific method?

- Has the theory been peer reviewed? The court recognized, however, that this is only one component of a greater assessment and wrote that this standard 'does not correlate with reliability… but submission to the scrutiny of the scientific community is a component of good science.'[13].

- What is the rate of error? This can give clues as to how the experimental standards are controlled.

- Is there general acceptance? Although the court rejected this as the "gold standard" it did acknowledge that this may be *one* useful factor when making an overall determination.

The Court specifically noted that these suggestions were not meant to be viewed as a definitive list of elements that make up admissible expert testimony. Rather, Blackmun wrote, 'the focus, of course must be solely on principles and methodology, not on the conclusions that they generate' [13]."[52]

Have your *Expert Report* peer reviewed. It will strengthen your position and enhance your ability to prevail at trial.

Keep in mind that the chief purpose of expert testimony is to allow "...the judge to be able to answer the question, how does this testimony help the jury resolve the case?"[53]

In today's litigious environment, the stakes for both plaintiffs and defendants in a case are quite high. Opposing counsel will do everything possible to discredit your work, and if that fails, will engage in character assassination of your person. You must be prepared for both possibilities, and this book will help you do just that.

In order that your Expert Report and contemplated oral testimony will be accepted by the court or hearing panel, you need to make certain you are qualified in every respect and that the credentials you present in your CV are accurate and complete. In addition, you need to make sure your written Expert Report and contemplated testimony are reliable and relevant to the case. Otherwise you run the risk of having your Expert Report and testimony rejected. One way you can help prevent this from happening is to have your Expert Report peer or third party reviewed.

Remember always to make arrangements early on to have your work product peer reviewed. This is something you don't want to do at the last minute. Make sure your peer reviewer has a copy of all the relevant materials you relied upon to prepare your Expert Report. Don't forget

---

52 Ibid, p. 2.
53 Ibid.

to include in that package a copy of your Expert Report. That is the document she will be analyzing.

Chapter XI

Giving a Deposition

To some lawyers all facts are created equal.
  -Justice Felix Frankfurter

Giving deposition testimony is an early litmus test as to the quality of your Expert Report. The Expert Report you prepared and what you say in deposition becomes foundational to your oral testimony to be given later at trial.

The scheduling of a deposition is formalized with the issue of a subpoena. Should you receive a subpoena to testify at a deposition, it is important you acknowledge receipt of the same in a timely fashion. You must confirm in writing to the subpoenaing authority that you are in receipt of the document and that you will appear at the location and on the date in which you are instructed to appear. If for whatever reason you cannot make an appearance, you must notify the authorities accordingly, and arrange to reschedule your appearance at a mutually convenient date.

Once a time and place for deposition testimony is agreed upon, you must start making preparation. You will need to get together with the trial lawyer who engaged you in the matter and begin to gather pertinent materials for your appearance. Those materials include: 1) an **Expert Report**, 2) a **CV** and 3) a **CV Certification Binder**. You should gather any other materials required of you for the deposition and described in the subpoena. You then need to schedule a time and place to meet with the trial lawyer assigned to the case in order to prepare for your upcoming testimony. Ideally, this should be the day before the hearing date.

Deposition is Formal Dress Rehearsal for Trial.

The taking of depositions in a lawsuit is a part of the discovery process. It provides opposing counsels the occasion to view ahead of time what testimony to expect at trial. Giving a deposition helps the testifying expert anticipate what to expect during cross-examination at trial.

You should come to the deposition well prepared. You need to ensure that you have all required documents with you in order to give an effective testimony. You must dress for the occasion. (See pages 21 and 22). Show up for your deposition well rested and on time.

Giving a Deposition – What to Expect

On the day of the deposition, the first item on the agenda is having you sworn in by the stenographer who will be archiving your testimony. It is then customary that you are presented with a check from opposing counsel reflecting payment for your appearance. The amount of the check should reflect your fee for testimony plus any travel or lodging expenses associated with your appearance.

It is opposing counsel's day. She will be taking your deposition. The lawyer who retained you in the matter, and who will be accompanying you at the deposition will be a spectator. Opposing counsel will typically begin with some administrative questions such as, "Do you have now an outstanding account balance with the engaging law firm who hired you to be an expert witness in this case?" He will be inferring that if indeed there are funds due you, somehow you may compromise your testimony just to get paid. A cheap shot yes - but one you can expect.

Opposing counsel may then ask you how you came to be retained in the matter. She may then verify that you are appearing in-accordance-with a subpoena and then verify you brought all materials which were requested. She may then ask if you brought any other materials in addition to those asked for in the subpoena.

Much can happen at a deposition. There is no set order of questioning, so be prepared for the unexpected. Answer all questions truthfully. **Under no circumstances must you ever lie.** "'Lying is the throwing away, and, as it were, the obliteration of one's dignity as a human being'."[54] If you don't know the answer to a question, just say so. Be professional at all times during the deposition.

Depositions usually start with a line of questioning, beginning with your Expert Report. A copy of this document will have been provided opposing counsel well before your deposition was scheduled. Opposing counsel will have had ample time to review your report and formulate her line of questioning prior to the deposition.

Oftentimes, opposing counsel will break from your Expert Report and turn to your CV, and begin asking questions about your credentials and your qualifications to testify at trial. Remember, opposing counsel is going to do everything possible to either: 1) have your testimony thrown out, 2) discredit you by engaging in character assassination or 3) turn you into her witness. This is where your CV Certification Binder will come in handy. But do stay alert. This can prove to be a tricky time during your deposition. It usually comes just before lunch break when you're hungry and could use some fresh air. He wants it this way – he wants to wear you down.

After lunch, opposing counsel will usually return to your Expert Report and begin to zero in on your areas that are at the heart of your testimony. She will want to know: 1) how you formulated your opinion in the matter, 2) what evidentiary standards were met for the formation of your opinion, 3) what was the basis of your opinion and 4) your contemplated use of charts and diagrams. Opposing counsel may posit a hypothetical question to you. Here she is trying to either turn you into her witness, or cause you to discredit your own testimony. I try to avoid answering hypothetical questions. They are set-ups. I usually respond by saying, "I'd like to give that some thought. There are a number of factors that I'd have to consider in order to answer the question effectively and as I sit here right now, I'm not prepared to do that."

At the end of the deposition, any matters that need to be resolved before trial or clarified are discussed. Those items are then archived in the transcript. The deposition is then concluded.

If at any time the session should get heated, ask for a break, collect yourself, and start again. One final reminder, under no circumstances

---

54   Arkes, Hadley. *First Things*. Princeton: Princeton University Press, 1986, p. 105.

should you ever let opposing counsel engage in character assassination. Bring a halt to that kind of behavior immediately. If opposing counsel doesn't stop, excuse yourself, get up and walk out of the deposition.

Chapter XII

Tales from the Hot Seat

> *One day tells its tale to another, and one night imparts knowledge to another.*
> —Psalm 19:2[55]

To know that your deposition went well is personally satisfying. To come to understand that your direct testimony at trial added value to the court in arriving at the right decision and that you handled cross-examination with dignity is professionally rewarding. To know that your overall performance scored points in helping your side win the case is gratifying. The price you pay to achieve this stature doesn't come easily.

Expert witness work is grueling.

The work that goes into the preparation of a quality Expert Report followed by flawless oral testimony at deposition and trial will 'stress test' the best of people. In the end, it is the personal satisfaction of accomplishment, recognition and financial reward that makes it all worthwhile.

Success comes with a price.

It is easy to talk about your 'wins' in the courtroom. It is not so easy to talk about one's unsuccessful appearances as an expert witness. You purchased this book to learn. You bought the book to hear what bad things might happen to you as an expert witness. You want to know what can go wrong at deposition or trial. You want to be able to benefit from others' mistakes. You want to be able to navigate the minefield successfully.

---

[55] *The* Book *of* Common Prayer. According to the use of *The Episcopal Church*. New York: The Church Hymnal Corporation, 1979, p. 606.

To ensure you get this information with transparency and have it told to you like it really is what follows are some:

Tales from the *Hot Seat*.

An Expert without an Expert Report

In the early 1990s, I was asked to be an expert witness in an employee contract lawsuit between a futures commission merchant (FCM) and two of the firm's associated persons (APs). The APs, as I recall, were related. The FCM was seeking monetary restitution from their two employees whereby the FCM was contending a breach of contract. I was asked to provide oral testimony in the case on behalf of the two APs who were the defendants in the lawsuit. The matter was heard before an NASD Arbitration panel.

The preparation phase took weeks to complete and went well past midnight - one day before the trial. There was no time to prepare an Expert Report. There was no time for me to be 'prepped' by the lawyer trying the case prior to the hearing.

The next morning, I flew to the location of the trial and later that day I began giving oral testimony before the arbitration panel. Absent the development of an Expert Report in the matter and not having been prepped by the trial lawyer the day before the hearing, surprisingly, my direct testimony went quite well. I was destroyed on cross-examination. I vowed never to let this happen again. And it hasn't. I have never appeared at trial without having prepared a first-rate *Expert Report*.

Always prepare *an Expert Report* before trial.

In addition to having constructed a first–rate Expert Report, you must insist on being prepped by the trial lawyer you are working for the day before your testimony is to be given. There can be compromises. If for whatever reason an Expert Report cannot be prepared and made available before deposition or trial testimony, or you can't be prepped ahead of time by the trial lawyer assigned to the case, cancel your appearance before the scheduled hearing date. Your professional reputation is at stake.

Last-Minute Expert

In another instance, I received a call one evening around 11:00 p.m. It was from a lawyer who told me that I had been referred to him by an attorney who I knew and had done litigation support work for in the past. The lawyer proceeded to tell me that he would be going to trial in three days and was in need of an expert to testify at that proceeding. He went on to say that the case involved wrongdoing in the trading of silver and gold futures contracts on the COMEX and what he wanted me to do was merely help educate the jury as to terms and procedures associated with the trading of commodity futures contracts. At first blush, the assignment sounded simple enough. Just make an appearance at the hearing, help educate the court and bring enlightenment to the jury. Seemingly, this would help the jury and the judge better understand the case and hopefully arrive at the right decision. *Not so fast.*

Had I accepted such an assignment, I would have opened myself up to all kinds of risk exposure. First, I was not familiar with the particulars of the case and had I accepted the assignment, I would have left myself wide open to a host of hypothetical questions from opposing counsel during cross-examination. That is to say, a clever lawyer could well have turned me into his expert. Should an assignment such as this come your way, you know the response – "Thanks for thinking of me. Good bye."

You may find this *tale* amusing.

You've Been Served

Out of the clear blue, I received a subpoena one day to appear for a deposition in a litigation matter. I had absolutely no idea of what this was about. A subpoena is a legal document and must be dealt with timely. Instantly, I began making inquiry into the matter. I discovered that my name (without my permission) had been placed by a lawyer on the expert witness list in the case. As the matter began to evolve through its formal litigation stages, whoever proffered my name had never taken the proper steps to have it removed from the witness list. Understandably, opposing counsel was interested in what I had to say in the matter and scheduled me for a deposition.

I contacted the lawyer who had the subpoena issued and explained that I had never been retained in the matter and that my name on the witness list was a mistake. Having listened to my explanation, he took the appropriate steps to have the subpoena quashed and my name removed from the witness list. As you appear more often in court cases, your CV and name will begin to surface. Don't be surprised if one day you receive a subpoena to make a court appearance in a case that you have zero knowledge about. Just give it time, this will happen to you. Be prepared to take swift action and remedy the problem. These are just a few tales from the *Hot Seat*. Stay tuned; there are more tales from the *Hot Seat* to come.

To get from here to there, requires hard work, perseverance and a proclivity for heightened attention to detail. It compels you to have a command of your particular academic discipline and work experience. You must have the ability to articulate complex ideas in simple terms to the jury. The uninitiated must be able to understand in plain terms your key points. That is to say, you must be able to explain complicated issues in simple terms. Finally, and most important, to be an effective expert witness, you must have a complete understanding as to how a courtroom works and how to be effective with the judge and jury. The following are some pointers which will help you better manage your courtroom appearance, thereby increasing your effectiveness as an expert witness.

You must be well prepared to give an effective *direct* testimony.

In terms of getting prepared for direct testimony, make sure the trial lawyer who sought your services as an expert witness has provided you ample time to do a thorough case formulation which includes: 1) the study of documents, 2) making analysis and 3) the preparation of an Expert Report. There must be sufficient time to make preparation for giving a deposition and later oral testimony at trial.[56] In terms of getting prepared to make oral testimony, I offer two important suggestions:

First, complicated matters may require days of oral testimony. I suggest you first do a "mock" trial. That is to say, you should arrange with the trial lawyer who hired you to do a "dress rehearsal." In this

---

56 Manuet, Thomas A. *Fundamentals of Trial Techniques.* Boston: Little Brown & Company, 1992, p. 71.

setting, the lawyer should practice his direct line of questioning. A second lawyer from the engaging law firm who you do not know should provide cross-examination. Second, videotape the mock trial. This will facilitate the critical evaluation of both direct testimony and cross-examination. It is better to make your mistakes at dress rehearsal than after the curtain has gone up on opening night.

This has been said before, but it's worth repeating, at deposition and trial you must be consistent and stay with your Expert Report. If new information should come to your attention after you have prepared your Expert Report, do not be concerned. You can always modify your report and include those materials in a revised document. Should this information come after you have given deposition, then merely update your Expert Report as need be and acknowledge the same at trial. This is not a *deal breaker*.

Just make sure this is accomplished and all applicable parties are notified in a timely fashion. You want to detonate all potential minefields early on. Don't wait and get caught off guard during cross-examination.

To be an effective expert witness you must learn how to read a hearing panel and jury. In the case of a trial, the first step is to do your homework on the presiding judge and gain knowledge of her background. Find out where she was born and raised. Determine where she went to college and law school. Try and gain as much information about her social and political leanings. This will help you assess where the judge may stand on a number of issues which could have an impact on your case. There are a number of directories which carry this information. In my opinion, the *Martindale-Hubbell Directory* is one of the best.[57]

At the end of the day, those who hear your testimony and rely on what you have to say to render a decision in the matter are people just like you and me. And of course, that is the case with the jury or arbitration hearing panel. Above all, they appreciate honesty and openness. They will regard your testimony highly if they feel you can be trusted and that you are there, first of all, to assist them in arriving at a fair and right decision. While you certainly have your lawyer's client's best interest at heart, your first job is to help the jury or arbitration panel as the case may be, reach the right decision.

---

57   Appendix E.

My last thoughts on giving direct testimony include keeping good eye contact with the hearing panel members, judge and jury. This doesn't mean to stare at the actors. This would cause terrible discontent between you and the panel, jury and judge. You certainly don't want this to happen. Good eye contact means confidence and friendliness, not some confrontational antics. That you don't need. By the way, this also applies when being cross-examined by opposing counsel. Use good eye contact - not a confrontational stare.

In some courtrooms, the witness chair is stationary. You can't turn it and face the judge or jury directly. If that's the case, seek out the location of the video camera in the courtroom. Most trials are videotaped for later viewing by the judge and her staff. When you want to make a strong point during your testimony, look right into that camera. The judge will perk-up when viewing your testimony after trail.

Be prepared for anything during cross-examination.

During the litigation process, cross-examination occurs in two instances. First, it takes place at deposition. After all, that's what depositions are all about. Deposition testimony gives opposing counsel an opportunity to see ahead of time, what you plan to say at trial. If you are able to survive that exercise, the second time you will be subjected to cross-examination is in the court room.

Opposing counsel in a lawsuit has one mission and that is to eliminate any possibility of you showing up for trial and giving oral testimony. He will use the deposition hearing to make that cut. His first approach will be an attempt to destroy the credibility of your Expert Report. If that fails, he will turn to your CV and make an attempt on your character. The stakes are high and the strategy is no-holds- barred poker. You must be prepared to play *hardball*.

At deposition, after the swearing in and the making of some preliminary opening comments, opposing counsel will begin with a review of your Expert Report. His first attempt will be to have you agree with as many of his observations made from your report as possible. The goal for him is to take your Expert Report, twist the outcomes of your findings and turn you into his witness. The next line of questioning will attempt to draw negative responses from your report. The goal here is to begin striping away, piece by piece, the themes in your report leading up to your conclusions. If opposing counsel perceives that he is not being effective in destroying your Expert Report as intended, then be prepared because he is going to come after you personally.

More tales from the *Hot Seat*.

Caught in a Litigation Crossfire

I had been retained by a law firm to provide litigation consultant services in a potential lawsuit. Some time later, I discoverd that my work product in the matter had fallen into the hands of an *adversary*. Should this happen to you, contact your personal attorney immediately and report the incident to the local bar association. Unauthorized disclosure of your work product compromises your intellectual property and makes you unnecessarily vulnerable when giving future testimony.

Never allow your proprietary work product to be disclosed to a third party unless directed by court order.

In another instance, I was involved in an action involving an AP registrant.[58] I was retained as an expert witness in the case. I developed a comprehensive Expert Report in anticipation of giving a deposition and later providing trial testimony in the matter. Shortly thereafter, a subpoena was issued to schedule my deposition in connection with my litigation consultant work in the case. The deposition hearing lasted seven hours. Two hours were devoted to the examination of my Expert Report. Using my CV, the opposing counsel spent the remaining five hours engaged in a series of questions of a personal nature.[59] Although rare, these things do happen and you must be prepared for the unexpected.

Here are some highlights from that performance.

Opposing counsel had somehow obtained parts of my proprietary work materials from an unrelated case. Among those materials, I had referenced the notion of 'judgment proof' in an e-mail. Opposing counsel zeroed in on that wording which I had written and asked me if that had something to do with "squirreling away funds for the defendant in that case" - or words to that effect. I was aghast at his question.

---

58   Appendix H.
59   Ibid.

I began to wonder "Can you make words mean *so* many different things?" And then I remembered, "The question is," said Humpty Dumpty, "which is to be master - that's all."[60] What I didn't do was counter with the *master's* response and explain that being "judgment proof" is a perfectly legal concept and is often sought out as an alternative to bankruptcy.[61]

There is a valuable lesson to be learned from this:

Have available at deposition and trial a comprehensive *CV Certification Binder.*

Now, I always bring with me to deposition and trial a most comprehensive and well-organized CV Certification Binder.

Not long after that deposition was given, I received a subpoena to appear for a videotaped deposition in another matter.[62]

This time however, I had compiled a comprehensive CV Certification Binder and brought it with me. During the opening remarks segment of the videotaped deposition, opposing counsel asked me if I had brought with me any materials other than those requested I bring to the hearing as described in the subpoena. I responded "Yes that I had with me a CV Certification Binder." The lawyer asked if he could see the binder. I produced the document as he requested. He looked through the CV Certification Binder and silently returned the document to me. Not once during that videotaped deposition did he ask me any questions about information listed on my Curriculum Vitae.

Litigation consultant and expert witness work can be challenging to say the least. The rewards are great, but you must be on your mark at all times. Your goal as an expert witness is to stay one step ahead of opposing counsel.

Some trial lawyers *can* be belligerent

In order to get their way, some highly trained trial lawyers will become quite belligerent and test your mettle. The questions will become fast pitch. You must be on guard at all times, thinking quickly, but yet responding slowly to each question with calmness and deliberation.

---

60   Carroll, Lewis. *Alice's Adventures in Wonderland and Through the Looking-Glass.* New York: Barnes & Noble Classics, 2004, p. 219.
61   Debtor-creditor.lawyers.com. 9/13/2009.
62   Appendix I.

Some lawyers are physically large people. They will try and use their physical stature to intimidate witnesses. Some play-act that they are a linebacker for the Pittsburgh Steelers. I have some advice for you. Don't let this type of lawyer get to you. You have an extensive background in the industry you are representing; otherwise your lawyer wouldn't have selected you to assist her with her trial. If your Expert Report is done to perfection, you have completed a mock trial dress rehearsal successfully, you have your CV Certification Binder with you, and you've been prepped by your trial lawyer the night before the hearing, you will be able to manage easily most situations that will arise during cross-examination. You'll do just fine.

It's when expert witnesses come to deposition or trial unprepared, that's when trouble begins. When experts appear arrogant and overly confident, that's when a skilled trial lawyer can often undermine the credibility of an expert and do great damage. Just be professional, carry yourself with confidence and dignity, and your testimony will be top drawer.

Keep all your testimony experiences consistent. Don't say something in one case, and then take a different stance in another matter, especially where the circumstances are the same. A good trial lawyer will find ways to get copies of your earlier testimony transcripts. Upon review, if she detects an inconsistency, you can rest assured it's going to come out at deposition and trial. This will put you on the defensive and it will be very difficult for you to regain your footing. You don't want to be put in that position. Your credibility begins to erode instantly and it's next to impossible for you to recover. The damage has been done.

I would like to return to your Expert Report for a moment. Beware of the trial lawyer who doesn't want you to craft such a document. His argument will be that he wants flexibility to meet unexpected happenings at deposition or during the trial. He will contend that you have vast knowledge and experience and he wants to be able to draw on those talents to meet unexpected challenges at trial. An Expert Report, he will argue, limits his ability to maneuver. And guess what? That's true.

At first blush, this rationale may flatter you and seem to stroke your ego. Let me tell you from the *hot seat* - forget it. What this trial lawyer really wants to do is to have the flexibility to manipulate your testimony if things begin to go bad for him during your deposition or at trial.

Don't fall for this ploy. You could well end up being the *scapegoat* for the lawyer who botched the trial. If the trial lawyer insists that you not prepare an Expert Report, that he wants flexibility in the courtroom, pass on the assignment.

In closing, do remember one thing:

Never surprise the trial lawyer who has engaged you in a litigation matter.

As the case formulation phase begins to develop and certain information begins to appear, pass along to counsel immediately, anything you find which could impact your case. That includes **bad** information a well as the **good**. Keep your testimony history consistent and always conduct yourself in a neutral and impartial manner. Work with materials and information objectively. Do your best to assist the hearing panel, jury and judge presiding over the case. Write a professional Expert Report. This document is foundational to your testimony at deposition and trial.

Most important, I hope you learned much from my personal experiences in the *Hot Seat*.

Chapter XIII

Conclusion

The law itself is on trial in every case as well as the cause before it.
                                        -Justice Harlan F. Stone

Trial work is tough stuff.

It requires extraordinary preparation on behalf of legal counsel. Expert testimony is only part of a bigger picture. It does however, play a key role in many cases. As a case develops and the trial date draws closer, the scheduling of depositions becomes crucial. The litigation atmosphere begins to get tense. Patience among all parties begins to wear thin. The expert witness will be in the thick of it all.

During the twenty-three years I was an expert witness, I was involved in forty-three lawsuits. Two of these cases were criminal matters. I was a non-testifying expert in seventeen cases and a testifying expert in twenty-six cases. I appeared in the: 1) Southern District of New York (Manhattan), 2) Southern District of Florida (Miami), 3) Southern District of Texas (Houston) and 4) Superior Court of California (Los Angles).

Of the twenty-six lawsuits where I gave expert testimony; in fifteen of those cases I represented the Defendant and ten cases I represented the Plaintiff. I was a fact witness in one matter. As to the twenty-six cases where I acted as a testifying expert, fifteen of those involved giving deposition and ten were providing testimony at trial. Eight awards were granted to the side I represented and in three instances, that was not the case. With respect to the remaining fifteen cases, the parties settled their differences either before the proceeding or sometime during the trial.

My twenty-three years as a litigation consultant and expert witness have caused me to come in contact with over one hundred trial lawyers in the United States. Many of these lawyers were extremely competent.

Some were not. Most all of them operated with integrity and dignity. The majority held to a code of high moral standards and ideals. A few were *corrupt*.

That being said, here are some reminders:

- Do **not** ever go to trial without an *Expert Report*.

- Never allow a law firm to produce your work product to an adversary unless directed to do so by court order. This kind of action borders on *unauthorized disclosure* and compromises your intellectual property. It provides for an open attack on your person at deposition and trial.

- Don't ever put yourself in a position of getting *lampooned at a deposition*. This can happen if you leave yourself exposed.

- Always have with you at deposition and trial a ***CV Certification Binder***. You just may get a question about an event which had taken place 25 years earlier. Since most people can't remember what they had for diner three days earlier, its extremely difficult for people to recall what happened a quarter century ago.

- Be prepared for the unexpected.

As a result of the many experiences talked about in the *Tales from the Hot Seat* chapter, I developed a list of **Do's** and **Don'ts** when acting as a litigation consultant and expert witness. I suggest you review this list at least twice. Review the list once before you accept an engagement, and review it a second time before you give either a deposition or oral testimony at trial.

Don't exaggerate to make your points.

Speak naturally and in easy to understand terms. You do not have to use simile and metaphor to make your points to the jury. And you certainly don't need to exaggerate your narrative to gain the jury's attention. By exaggerating points, you may easily come across as being a phony. You lose credibility doing that.

Don't minimize bad information.

Tackle bad information head-on. As soon as information that could be adverse to your case comes to your attention, pass it on immediately to the trial lawyer. Don't dilute the information. Let the trial lawyer develop her own strategy on how to handle it.

Don't appear arrogant.

Even if you have just been awarded the Nobel Prize for a breakthrough in your particular area of expertise, stay humble. Don't wear your accomplishments on your sleeve. E. Digby Baltzell (1915-1996) was Emeritus Professor of History and Sociology at the University of Pennsylvania. In his book, *Philadelphia Gentlemen*, Baltzell describes the aplomb of a *lady* and a *gentleman* which you should try to emulate.[63]

Do appear professional at deposition and trial. **Do** carry yourself with a lady-like and gentlemanly-like dignity. Your demeanor will speak for itself.

Don't be combative with the opposing trial lawyer.

Always treat opposing counsel with dignity and professional respect. If opposing counsel begins to get belligerent, the lawyer representing the case will in most cases intercede and put a stop to that type of behavior. This typically happens at deposition or before arbitration hearing panels. This sort of action is usually flushed out before a court trial commences. However, should opposing counsel begin to get rude during any appearance and the trial lawyer representing your side remains passive, by all means get feisty and fight back. You have a reputation to protect. Tell opposing counsel you find his behavior and line of questioning to be ungentlemanly, and if the proceeding (deposition testimony) is to continue, that a change in direction is necessary. Otherwise you will cease giving testimony. Ask for a break, let all parties calm down, regain their composure and restart the deposition fresh.

When the deposition resumes, chances are it will take on a whole new tone. Opposing counsel will learn something in the process - he can't push your button at trial. And don't forget, stay with your **Expert Report.**

---

[63] Baltzell, E. Digby. *Philadelphia Gentlemen*. Glencoe: The Free Press, 1958, pp. 384 – 389.

Don't talk in technical terms or use your particular industry's jargon.

Always communicate your technical information to the jury in plain English. Use easy to understand terms. Remember, a jury is comprised of people from all walks of life. The effective expert witness must be able to touch the hearts and minds of all individuals seated in the jury box.

Don't let the opposing attorney cause you to lose your temper.

When giving testimony, always remain calm and dignified. Always retain your personal and professional demeanor.

Don't ever guess at giving an answer to a question from opposing counsel.

If asked a question, and you don't know the answer, say so. Just say, "I don't know." You are not expected to know everything pertaining to your field of expertise.

Don't hold yourself out as an *Expert* in a field you are NOT expert in.

Only offer your professional services as a litigation consultant and expert witness in the area you have a command of the academic discipline and related work experience. Even if a professional field might be indirectly related, but is **NOT** directly related, pass on the assignment. For example, if your area of expertise is listed securities, be careful about accepting a case involving futures, swaps or derivative instruments. Although they may well have the touchstone of commonality, their structure and uses are different. Remember, the securities markets are regulated by the SEC and the futures markets are regulated by the CFTC. These two markets operate with two very distinct sets of written federal regulations.

Do be an *Expert* in your professional field only.

There is no room for a dilettante in professional litigation support and expert witness work. People who are parties to a litigation matter deserve the best legal representation they can get. Most often large sums of money are at stake. At other times, people's lives are at risk. In terms of qualification to act as an expert witness in a litigation matter, there is absolutely no room for compromise.

Do be courteous to all parties at all times.

"And I did not open them for him; and it was *courtesy* to treat him boorishly."[64] "Loud and inconsiderate behavior in public places ... has always been considered bad manners because it does not take into consideration the feelings and needs of others."[65] Remember, the courtroom belongs to the judge. This is her domain. Show respect for her, by showing respect for her courtroom and those who may be occupying it during the trial.

Do be professional.

"Be thou familiar but by no means vulgar."[66] Always maintain high ethical standards. Hold to the moral high ground. Never compromise yourself.

Do answer the questions asked.

During cross-examination, if you do not know the answer to a question posed to you by opposing counsel, just say so. You can certainly ask opposing counsel to rephrase a question. That is perfectly acceptable. But don't attempt to reword the question yourself in order to arrive at some sort of answer. Never reach for a response to a question, and that goes for direct testimony as well as cross-examination.

Do be firm.

Never let opposing counsel beat you up while giving deposition or testimony at trial. This is **NOT** professional. This type of behavior is **NOT** productive to the legal process at hand. Most often, the chairperson of the arbitration hearing panel or the judge in a court case will halt such behavior. In the event this does **NOT** occur, step in and protect yourself.

---

64   Alighieri, Dante. *Inferno*. Oxford: Oxford University Press, 1996, p. 523.
65   Vanderbilt, p. 314.
66   Shakespeare, William. *Hamlet*. New York: Barnes & Noble Classics, 2003, p. 44.

At deposition, tell opposing counsel if he continues his obnoxious behavior, you will halt the deposition. If it is an arbitration hearing or trial, ask the presiding officer to intercede on your behalf. You have every right to protect your reputation.

<u>Do</u> speak in plain English.

Make complicated concepts and materials easy to understand for the jury or hearing panel as the case may be. Use graphs, charts and tables to make your points. Visual aids are often quite useful when conveying difficult pieces of information to others. People think in symbolism, and visual tools are quite helpful.

<u>Do</u> tell the TRUTH always.

Don't *reach* when answering a question. Answer the question in a straight forward manner. Keep the response to a minimum as to **NOT** confuse the jury. Remember the old adage ***KISS***- keep it simple, stupid. Recall George Washington's advice to the American people in his *Farewell Address* to the nation in 1796 -"honesty is always the best policy."[67]

Your performance at deposition and trial makes lasting marks on your professional reputation. If you are to have staying power as a litigation consultant and expert witness, this one thought needs to be paramount in your mind at all times.

Some years ago, I was giving testimony at a trial. During the break, I overheard a lawyer remark to his colleague, "Experts are like old bulls: once you've used them, you are done with them." Most lawyers I worked with over the past twenty-three years have treated me with respect. That comment I overheard however, gave me an early wake-up call as to how the litigation process really works. Again, it is nothing personal; it's just the way it is. Therefore, it is incumbent on you to stand your ground at all times. Never, ever, compromise your ethics. Never compromise your professional status or your moral fortitude. Your job is to be impartial when developing your Expert Report, relying only on the materials provided to you by the engaging counsel and used as evidence in support of your findings

---

67 The Avalon Project: Washington's Farewell Address 1796 last modified on: 02/02/2008. Copyright 1996 The Avalon Project at Yale Law School.

and conclusions in your report. To have staying power as an expert witness, you must maintain a solid professional reputation within your industry grouping. The quickest way to lose your stature is to fall on the sword for a lawyer and his case. Never do it. It's not worth it. Trust me when I say this.

Epilogue

I think the first duty of society is justice.
                                                -Alexander Hamilton

Americans are truly blessed with a wonderful judicial system established by the *Founding Fathers* and provided for in the *Constitution of the United States of America*. This judicial mechanism went into effect in 1789. For over 220 years the judicial branch of government has provided the body politic a forum to settle disputes. The American legal system is not perfect, but when compared to the alternatives, it is the most appealing.

The jury system in the United States brings an extraordinary balance to the legal process. For those who are on trial, it gives a degree of comfort to know that especially in criminal matters, the notion of the presumption of innocence until proven guilty is the governing principle in America. Judges and hearing panels want to administer justice fairly and impartially. They realize that the very foundation upon which the American legal system is built rests squarely on the public's continued confidence in their ability to administer justice fairly. Should this trust disintegrate, the risk is quite real that the populace would seek a new legal system by forming a new government. This raises a very real concern for American society, which for the most part, operates today in chaos and whirl. The nation's economic base is in long-term decline. Its political stability is at best, fragile.

Part of administering the justice system in America requires that various legal instruments be kept safe in the legal system's toolbox. One of those tools is the litigation consultant and expert witness. Courts have said that expert testimony can be most helpful in arriving at a just verdict.[68] The experts most sought after are the ones who have compiled an impressive track record which includes representation for both plaintiffs and defendants. In addition, lawyers look for experts who have a varied experience testifying before arbitration panels as well as

---

68   Appendix F. Grady, pp. 1-4.

court forums. Experience testifying before a jury is especially attractive to have on your CV.

Nearly every industry is subject to litigation exposure in one way or another. Some industries however, seem to be more prone to having a lawsuit filed against them than others. Those industries include: 1) the medical profession, 2) construction, 3) real estate, 4) computer science, 5) banking, 6) stock brokerage, 7) commodities, and 8) general workplace misconduct.

To qualify as an expert witness, a person must have a command of a particular work-station environment. Qualifying factors include years of successful experience in an industry and a heightened academic understanding of the mechanics and workings of that industry. A solid qualifying factor would be having years of work experience in the federal or state government. Ideally, a potential expert witness would have more than one of these qualifying factors.

Successful litigation consultants and expert witnesses look and act the part. In a word, they look *conservative*. Women and men who expect to rise to the highest level in the litigation support profession need to make sure their outward appearance is attractive and lasting. Remember, different colors send different messages to those engaged in the litigation process. Don't forget, first impressions are lasting impressions. Most importantly, an expert's appearance should not distract the judge, jury or panel from the testimony.

You can be the best expert witness in the world, but if no one knows you exist, what good is it? You need to be marketing constantly your litigation support credentials.

The most valuable marketing piece in your toolbox is your **Curriculum Vitae (CV)**. Your CV is your handshake. You need to have a current CV on the desk of all top-drawer trial attorneys who practice in your particular field of expertise. There are other ways you can market your litigation support credentials.

You can write journal articles. You can serve as a panelist on arbitration panels. You should attend industry related conferences and seminars. You should accept all public speaking engagements when asked. To be successful, it is critical that you stay in the public eye. There is an old saying, *out of sight, out of mind*. You never want to be 'out of sight.'

Only accept litigation consultant and expert witness assignments from law firms. Never contract directly with a party that has filed a lawsuit, or who is being sued. Scope your assignment with the engaging law firm in phases. Ask the trial lawyer who has hired you, to arrange to have each phase of the litigation project funded prior to the commencement of the next phase of work. Ensure that your ***Engagement Letter*** includes, among other things, your fee schedule. Make sure the Engagement Letter has a clause that prohibits disclosure of your work product to any third party, except of course, when directed by a court. Your *intellectual property* is valuable. Your approach to litigation consultant work has a nature of *propriety*. If a law firm breaches this trust, your professional credentials will be compromised. Never let this happen.

Remember; never attend a trial with an outstanding financial balance due. Never go to trial if the final phase of the litigation preparation process has not been paid in total. You may be asked this question in cross examination; 'have you been paid in full for your services which you have provided in this case?' If you give a negative response, opposing counsel may well attempt to lampoon your testimony. He may well begin to attack your testimony as biased in order for you to gain favor from the lawyer you are working for in order to get paid. It's a *dirty tricks* tactic, but it is used often to discredit expert witness testimony.

Always keep in mind that a trial lawyer's job is to represent his or her client with utmost vigor. The goal is to win the case on behalf of the client at all costs. Litigation consultants and expert witnesses are nothing more than tools which are a part of the trial lawyer's litigation toolbox. You must be on guard at all times to protect your professional reputation. Keep the moral high ground and never compromise your ethical standards.

Never, ever, fall on the sword for a lawyer and his case.

It's not worth it. You have only your name and professional reputation to rely on for future litigation support work. You have to protect this valuable asset if you expect to have staying power as a litigation consultant and expert witness.

The ***Expert Report*** is the single most important document you will develop as a litigation consultant. It is foundational and becomes logocentric to your testimony at deposition and trial. The Expert Report defines the boundaries of your testimony. The content of your report will be relied upon by the jury in rendering a final decision in the matter. This document must be *first class*. It must be developed and written to perfection. Most important, it must be accurate and be displayed in a highly professional manner.

Beware of any lawyer who doesn't want you to craft an Expert Report. His motive is simple. If the trial starts going badly, he will be able to steer you in a direction you are not prepared to go in, merely to salvage the case. This can damage your professional reputation, maybe even permanently. Never allow yourself to become a *scapegoat* in a case.

Most top-notch lawyers who are associated with marquee law firms recognize the importance of having an expert witness craft a state-of-the-art Expert Report. Lawyers who enjoy a solid reputation within their legal profession understand well the role of an expert witness and the importance of presenting to the court a quality Expert Report. The majority of lawyers will treat you with dignity and respect. Premier trial lawyers will not go to trial with their expert witnesses without them first having prepared an Expert Report and have it in hand. But just in case you are unlucky, and run into that one in a thousand lawyer who, for whatever reason, doesn't want you to prepare an Expert Report, you will know exactly what to do. Pass on the assignment with a cordial, 'Thanks for thinking of me.'

Always go into a deposition or trial well prepared. Rehearse your testimony in a mock trial setting. Videotape your performance and later have the engaging lawyer critique your presentation. Always insist that you are 'prepped' the day before giving deposition or trial testimony. Come to the deposition and trial confident and carry a professional demeanor about you. Always answer the question being asked of you and never guess at the answer. If you don't know the answer to a question, say so. Never reach for an answer. Try not to answer the preverbal *hypothetical* question. These are set-up questions to turn you into the opposing counsel's witness. Just tell opposing counsel that you are not very good at dealing with hypothetical questions and put an end to it.

Never compromise your *ethical standards.*

If you came away from reading this book by gaining just one good idea, then it was worth your investment. I wish you great success as a litigation consultant and expert witness. You will achieve stardom in the litigation support arena if you do just three things: 1) seek perfection in your work, 2) conduct yourself at all times in a professional manner and 3) always maintain the moral high ground.

Appendices

Appendix A – The Financial Meltdown of 2008.
Appendix B – Sample Curriculum Vitae.
Appendix C – Sample Engagement Letter.
Appendix D – Sample Expert Report.
Appendix E – Litigation Forums, Legal and Regulatory Reference Listings.
Appendix F – Samuel Peltz vs. SHB Commodities, Inc.
Appendix G – U.S. Commodity Futures Trading Commission vs. Anthony Dizona, *et al*. Civil Action H-05-332.
Appendix H – U.S. Commodity Futures Trading Commission vs. Todd J. Delay. Civil Action 05CV5619.
Appendix I – U.S. Commodity Futures Trading Commission vs. Cromwell Financial Services, Inc., *et al*. Civil Action 05CV210-JD.

Appendix A

The Financial Meltdown of 2008

> *Banking may well be a career from which no man really recovers.*
>
> -John Kenneth Galbraith

In March 2008, disruptions began to appear in the United State's financial system. According to George Soros, "the municipal bond market fell apart (and) credit spreads continued to widen..."[69] The New York based investment firm Bear Stearns "came under suspicion as a counterparty" to certain financial transactions.[70] On March 20, 2008 "Bear Stearns was forced into the hands of JP Morgan at $2 a share."[71] On September 15, 2008, the New York based investment banking firm Lehman Brothers "was allowed to go into bankruptcy..."[72] These two developments ignited a global financial contagion and ushered in the Great Recession of the 21st century.

In 1929, the Bank of the United States was a privately owned bank headquartered in New York City. It was not a U.S. federal government bank as the name miscues. Ostensibly, the Bank of the United States had leveraged depositors' funds using mortgages as collateral. In the fall of 1929, the stock market in the U.S. crashed and housing prices began to tumble. As a result, the Bank of the United States "was in pretty poor shape."[73] On December 11, 1930 the New York State superintendent of banking closed the Bank of the United States."[74] The Great Depression of the 1930s had just begun.

---

69   Soros, pp. 138-139.
70   Ibid, p. 140.
71   Ibid, p. 141.
72   Ibid, p. 158.
73   Meltzer, Allan H. *A History of the Federal Reserve. Volume 1: 1913-1951.* Chicago: The University of Chicago Press, 2003, p. 324.
74   Ibid, p. 323.

The credit bubble was all about leverage.[75]

Both the Great Depression of the 1930s and the Great Recession of the 21st century have been caused by banks' leveraging their balance sheets and related involvement with real estate investments and their declining values. One feature that makes the Great Recession of the 21st century different and potentially more devastating from the Great Depression of the 1930s is that the current financial crisis has in large part been caused by banks and stock brokerage firms trading lethal investment products commonly referred to as swaps and derivative instruments.

As of June 2008, the Bank for International Settlements (BIS) estimates the gross market value of over-the-counter (OTC) derivative and swap contracts to be $20 trillion.[76] The BIS places the notional amount of OTC derivative and swap products outstanding at $684 trillion.[77] For the year 2008, the World Bank reported the world's Gross Domestic Product (GDP) to be $60.1 trillion.[78] That is to say, for the year 2008, the notional amount of OTC swap and derivative products outstanding was **ten times** the entire world's GDP. At the heart of the current global economic crisis and financial meltdown is the trading of toxic swap and derivative instruments by major international banks and stock brokerage firms. This development has put much of the free world on the brink of monetary collapse. In the April 13, 2009 issue of *Barron's*, "Billionaire investor George Soros is quoted as saying on Reuters Financial television, 'The banking system as a whole is basically insolvent'."[79]

Much of America's businesses and governments have become decadent and corrupt. This resulted in the nation's banking system collapsing in September 2008. This financial calamity has in turn caused the country's economy to become shattered. As a result, the nation's citizenry has suffered horrendous personal financial injury. These conditions provide for the need of highly skilled personnel to help: 1) restore the nation's economy to equilibrium and 2) make financial restitution to those innocent victims who suffered financial loss due

---

75 Ishikawa, p. 21.
76 www.bis.org/statistics/derstats.htm.
77 Ibid.
78 www.worldbank.org.
79 *Barron's*. April 13, 2009, p. 14.

to the unlawful behavior by people who were in positions of power, influence and fiduciary trust.

In July 2005, Bernard Ebbers, CEO of WorldCom, was sentenced to 25 years in federal prison for engineering an $11 billion accounting fraud. On October 23, 2006, Jeffrey Skilling, CEO of Enron, was sentenced to 24 years in federal prison for securities and corporate fraud violations which resulted in the largest corporate bankruptcy in U.S. history.

On March 12, 2009, Bernard L. Madoff pled guilty to an eleven-count criminal complaint admitting to have defrauded thousands of investors of "$50 billion."[80] This has been reported to be the largest investor fraud ever perpetrated by one individual. The United States Attorney's Office in New York City reported that "United States District Judge Denny Chin sentenced Madoff to serve 150 years in prison."[81] According to an article in the *New York Times,* Wednesday, November 4, 2009, columnist Diana B. Henriques reported that "…Madoff's longtime accountant … admitted in federal court that he produced the rubber-stamp audits that allowed Mr. Madoff to conceal his enormous Ponzi scheme from regulators for nearly 20 years."[82]

That same day in *The New York Times,* writer Damien Cave reported "… a Florida judge (had) placed (a Florida) law firm in receivership."[83] The article went on to say that "…federal authorities began investigating whether" investors had been defrauded of up to $400 million in "a Ponzi scheme based on selling legal settlements."[84]

According to a column which appeared in *Barron's* on Monday, October 26, 2009 the co-founder and head of the Galleon Group hedge fund has been "arrested on insider-trading charges."[85] This "is another black eye for the hedge-fund industry" the article reported.[86] Another matter involving *insider trading* was reported on Friday, November 6,

---

80 Soros, p. 163.
81 www.usdoj.gov. 8/4/2009.
82 Henriques, Diana B. Plea From Madoff Accountant May Lead to Tax Cases. *The New York Times.* November 4, 2009, p. B2.
83 Cave, Damien. Fraud Accusations Against Florida Lawyer Set Off a Race to Return Donations. *The New York Times.* November 4, 2009, p. A12.
84 Ibid.
85 Sullivan, Tom. Hedge Funds Underperform This Year. *Barron's.* October 26, 2009, p. 44.
86 Ibid.

2009 in *USA Today*. Writing for that newspaper, columnists Kevin McCoy and Laura Petrecca reported "…civil and criminal charges (had been filed) in a dramatic expansion of the largest insider-trading investigation in at least a generation."[87] The article went on to say "the alleged conspirators were charged on secret wiretap evidence and on information from at least five cooperating witnesses who allegedly got payoffs for passing inside information and have pleaded guilty."[88]

The unbridled use of highly leveraged swap and derivative products by banks and investment firms, coupled with crooked behavior by a number of Wall Street operators have left financial wreckage and debris on a scarred American socioeconomic and political landscape. Victims include: 1) countless members of the nation's citizenry, 2) corporate and state pension plans, 3) mutual funds, 4) trust company clients, 5) insurance companies, 6) non-U.S. financial institutions and 7) entire nations such as Iceland, "Dubai and Greece."[89]

Nancy Cavender says that "…overtolerance … (blinds us) to the defects and foibles of our own group and its members."[90] The American public's patience with Wall Street and Washington is running thin. The days of *overtolerance* are rapidly coming to an end. The public is in the process of demanding responsibility and accountability of its financial executives and federal government officials for their behavior and actions. Persons in positions of power, influence and control over the nation's well-being will be held to a higher standard of ethical conduct, moral behavior and adherence to the law in the years to come. For those who fail to meet those tenets, the public will demand that they be removed from their positions, prosecuted and sent to jail. The days of cover-up and federal government bailouts are rapidly coming to an end.

Cleveland Amory (1917-1998) was a 20th century author and social historian. In his book *Who Killed Society*, Amory contends that for the most part *café society* and *celebrity status* killed American gentility.[91] I

---

87 McCoy, Kevin and Petrecca, Laura. Insider trading bust digs deep. *USA Today*. November 6, 2009, p. 2A.
88 Ibid.
89 *The Economist*. Dubai's debt cliffhanger. December 19th 2009-January 1st 2010, pp. 89 and 128.
90 Cavender, p. 127.
91 Amory, Cleveland. *Who Killed Society?* New York: Harper & Brothers, Publishers, 1960, pp. 107-188.

argue that it was institutional decay, corporate greed and corruption at the federal and state government levels that have led to America's societal and financial destruction.

In the aftermath of the Crash of 2008, Sorkin is skeptical that Wall Street has learned its lesson. In his book *Too Big to Fail,* he says, "While the financial crisis destroyed careers and reputations ... it also left the survivors with a genuine sense of invulnerability ..."[92] He concludes by noting that what is "Still missing in the current environment is a genuine sense of humility."[93] If Sorkin's observations are correct, it will be a tragedy for the socioeconomic and political well-being of America.

In the not too distant future the nation's body politic will rise up and demand from their federal government representatives a complete and transparent accounting of what happened and who caused the 2008 collapse of America's banking and investment brokerage system. If the nation's citizenry is "to remain outside a phallocentric financial system 'is to leave it intact; to remain only within its terms ... (or) risk absorption'. "[94] The United States cannot afford to be absorbed permanently into an already corrupt and seriously broken financial system. The building of a new financial paradigm for America is essential. This endeavor will require the services of litigation consultants grounded with an expertise in finance, corporate governance and federal government regulation. That is to say, litigation consultants will come to assist the American people in "producing meaning (to Wall Street) rather than passively consuming it."[95]

Alfred Adler (1870-1937) was a medical doctor and psychologist. He founded the school of *individual psychology.* In his book *The Individual Psychology of Alfred Adler,* he discusses the notion of the "superiority complex."[96] Adler identifies the superiority complex as being "a compensation for the inferiority [feeling] complex."[97] He continues by saying, "The superiority complex is one of the ways which a person with

---

92 Sorkin, p. 538.
93 Ibid, p. 539.
94 Brooks, Ann. *Postfeminisms.* London: Routledge, 1997, p. 75.
95 Ibid, p. 142.
96 Adler, Alfred. *The Individual Psychology of Alfred Adler.* New York: Harper Torchbooks, 1964, p. 260.
97 Ibid.

an inferiority [feeling] complex may use as a method of escape from his difficulties."⁹⁸

We had moved on to hurting others in our quest for self-preservation.⁹⁹

Wall Street bankers cannot blindly escape from their financial difficulties and corporate responsibilities. They cannot shelve toxic assets on their balance sheets in sempiternity.¹⁰⁰ Financial executives cannot expect to seek cover and operate "… under new U.S. guidelines that are more forgiving of battered (commercial mortgages) values … in order to avoid bigger loses" forever.¹⁰¹ That sort of thinking is illusory.

As a result of the global financial crisis of 2008, the American public has lost enormous amounts of money. As events begin to unfold surrounding that calamity, the nation's citizenry will demand monetary restitution as a result of funds lost and punishment for those who brought about the worst financial debacle since the Great Depression.

Immanuel Kant (1724-1804) was an 18th century philosopher who "taught at the University of Konigsberg."¹⁰² He argued that "ethics is not contingent but absolute…based not on feeling but on reason."¹⁰³ Kant held that "punishment does public justice."¹⁰⁴ America will be caught in a perdurable cycle of litigation well into the second decade of the 21st century. Citizens will come to "rely on the legal process … to vindicate their wrongs."¹⁰⁵ In that connection, the complexities "stemming from the credit and financial crisis" will give rise for the demand of knowledgeable and experienced litigation consultants and expert witnesses who are well versed in the dynamic world of finance.¹⁰⁶

---

98   Ibid.
99   Ishikawa, p. 7.
100 Hall, Kevin G. New Rules to Affect Valuation of Toxic Assets. *Union-Tribune.* April 2, 2009.
101 Wei, Lingling and Grant, Peter. Banks Hasten to Adopt New Rules. *The Wall Street Journal.* November 11, 2009, p. C1.
102 Pojman, p. 495.
103 Ibid, p. 496.
104 Ibid, p. 649.
105 Ibid, p. 650.
106 Efrati, Amir. U.S. Loses Bear Fraud Case. *The Wall Street Journal.* November 11, 2009, p. A1.

APPENDIX B

SAMPLE CURRICULUM VITAE

Front Cover Page

Allison P. Wainwright
123 Carriage Street
Brooklyn Heights, NY 12345

Telephone: (212) 123-1234
Cell phone: (917) 234-5678
E-mail: awainwright@xyz.xxx

FOREIGN LANGUAGES

French – Fluent

PROFESSIONAL ASSOCIATIONS

Chartered Financial Analyst Society of New York – Member

REGISTRATIONS AND LICENSES

Chartered Financial Analyst – 2005
FINRA Series 24 Examination – 2000
FINRA Series 12 Examination – 2000
FINRA Series 3 Examination – 2000
FINRA Series 7 Examination – 2000

PROFESSIONAL EXPERIENCE

Assistant Portfolio Manager 2005 - Present
The Pension Plan
123 Park Avenue
New York, NY

Senior Analyst 2003 - 2005
Venture Mutual Fund
1 Wall Street
New York, NY

Associate Analyst 2002 – 2003
ABC Bank
23 Walnut Street
Philadelphia, PA

Junior Analyst 2000 – 2002
ABC Bank
23 Walnut Street
Philadelphia, PA

PROFESSIONAL DEVELOPMENT

Advanced Management Program – Certificate (2008)
Yale University
New Haven, CT

MILITARY

Honorable Discharge – 1998
United States Navy Commissioned Officer – 1995

EDUCATION

The Wharton School – MBA (1998 - 2000)
University of Pennsylvania
Philadelphia, PA

Bryn Mawr College – AB (1995)
Bryn Mawr, PA

1. ARTICLES

1.02 Wainwright, Allison P. <u>Investment Management for the 21st Century.</u> New York: *Finance Magazine.* March 9, 2009.

1.01 _____. <u>The Financial Crisis of 2008.</u> New York: *The Wall Street Journal.* December 31, 2008.

1.00 _____. <u>The Portfolio Manager</u>. Washington, DC: The Research Group, inc. June 31, 2006.

2. CONFERENCES

2.00 Wainwright, Allison P. Association of the Bar of the City of New York. **The Fiduciary Responsibility of the Portfolio Manager.** New York: September 31, 2005

3. NEWSPAPER AND PERIODICALS

3.00 Wainwright, Allison P. <u>Hedge Funds and the Crash of 2008.</u> New York: *The New York Times.* February 30, 2009.

AWARDS

United States Navy Commendation Medal

Appendix C

Sample Engagement Letter

This letter confirms your engagement by **[Name of Law Firm]** on behalf of our client **[Name of Client]** to assist us in connection with the above captioned matter. The lawsuit raises issues regarding **[Nature of the Complaint, State Law(s) allegedly violated and/or a summary of the crime(s) committed]**. This letter sets forth the terms of your engagement.

Nature of Engagement

In connection with the lawsuit, you will assist **[Name of Law Firm]** in investigating, reviewing and analyzing the sufficiency of **[Here state the particulars of the case and your specific involvement desired]**. You will undertake such projects mutually agreed to as may be authorized by **[Name of Law Firm]** and generally consult with, advise and assist **[Name of Law Firm]** in connection with the lawsuit and with other compliance matters which may arise from time to time.

Compensation

Your fees will be based on time expended plus reasonable travel, lodging, postage, communication and other out-of-pocket expenses. You shall be entitled to compensation at your standard hourly rate of **[Insert your hourly rate]** for time performing your responsibilities under this agreement.

It is contemplated that, from time to time, such responsibilities may require you to spend time traveling. In connection with any such travel, you shall be entitled to reimbursement for travel expenses that you reasonably and necessarily incur. All travel arrangements shall be pre-approved by **[Name of Law Firm]**. You will also be entitled to reimbursement for out-of-pocket expenses reasonably and necessarily incurred by you in connection with the performance of your responsibilities.

You will render invoices concerning this matter on a monthly basis. The invoices must include, at a minimum, itemized task and time detail. The invoices should be addressed to: **[Here insert the name of the lawyer who engaged you as a litigation consultant and his or her professional address including the name of the Law Firm].** The client has advised us that she or he agrees with this commitment.

Prohibited Activities

It is agreed that you shall not provide any services to: 1) any person or entity other than the client in connection with the lawsuit and 2) any person or entity that has asserted or proposes to assert in any other proceeding, litigation, or other matter any position antagonistic to that of the client.

Confidentiality

In connection with **[Name of Law Firm]** engagement of you, it is agreed that all communications between you and **[Name of Law Firm]** shall be regarded as confidential. In order for you to carry out your responsibilities under this agreement, it may be necessary for **[Name of Law Firm]** to disclose to you their legal theories, other privileged information, and attorney work product, and for the client, and his employees, agents, and/or representatives, to disclose to you other confidential information. Accordingly, it is agreed that before, during and after the period of this engagement, you will use such information solely for purposes of this engagement and will not disclose any privileged information, attorney work product, opinions, facts, data, or other confidential information disclosed to you in the course of your engagement to any person or entity including persons, businesses or instrumentalities of the government to whom disclosure has not been authorized in writing by **[Name of Law Firm]**. Nothing in this agreement, however, shall be construed as prohibiting disclosure pursuant to valid court order or other legal process.

All communications by you in connection with your responsibilities under this agreement shall be addressed to: **[Name of the engaging lawyer, his or her title and the name and address of the Law Firm].** All documents and other materials generated or prepared by you in connection with your activities under this engagement, including, but not limited to, e-mails and invoices shall be marked **"Privileged** and Confidential." All such documents and materials shall remain or become property of **[Name of the Law Firm]**. You agree that, before, during or after the period of your engagement, you will not disclose to any person other than **[Name of Law Firm]** any documents or other materials provided to you, or generated or prepared by or for you in connection with your engagement, unless disclosure to that person has been authorized in writing by **[Name of Law Firm]**. You may disclose such documents and materials to persons employed by or associated with you, provided that they agree to be bound by and abide by the confidentiality provisions of this agreement.

If any person or entity to whom disclosure has not been authorized in writing by **[Name of Law Firm]** requests, subpoenas, or otherwise seeks to obtain any theories, opinions, facts, data, information, documents, or other materials in your possession, custody or control that have been disclosed or provided to you, or generated or prepared by or for you in connection with this engagement, you shall immediately inform **[Name of Law Firm]** and at our expense, take such legal action deemed necessary or appropriate to resist disclosure of such theories, opinions, facts, data, information, documents or other materials. Except for measures requiring immediate action to preserve the status quo, you shall consult with **[Name of Law Firm]** prior to taking any legal action or making any decision in connection with such legal action, and shall pay all legal fees and expenses you incur as a result of such legal action. This shall not be construed to prohibit disclosure pursuant to a valid court order or other valid legal process.

Notwithstanding the above, **[Name of Law Firm]** will not make available or disclose any of your work product to any party without your prior written approval. Should **[Name of Law Firm]** contemplate such action, you will be provided the contemplated materials for review, and redact those portions you deem critical to protect your intellectual property and the integrity of your proprietary work product. Only those documents mutually agreed upon in advance, and in writing, will be provided to any third party.

Return of Materials

Except to the extent that **[Name of Law Firm]** agrees in writing, and upon termination or expiration of this agreement, you shall deliver to **[Name of Law Firm]** all documents and other materials, including all copies thereof, which have been provided to you in connection with your work pursuant to this agreement, and regardless of authorship, which embody or disclose in any way thereon, opinions, facts, data, information, documents or other materials disclosed or provided to you before and during this engagement, or have been prepared or are in the process of being prepared by you in connection with the engagement.

Termination

The engagement described above will end at the earlier of our termination of the engagement, or your withdrawal. All of your obligations under this agreement shall survive the termination and expiration of this agreement.

Closing Matters

The terms of this engagement cover your services rendered to date and thereafter. If any provision of this agreement is declared invalid or unenforceable, no other provision of this agreement is affected and all other provisions shall remain in full force and effect.

This agreement shall be subject and governed by the laws of the **[Enter the name of the state where the engaging Law Firm is located]** and any disputes arising from it shall be subject to mandatory arbitration under the auspices of the American Arbitration Association **[at a location nearest to both parties]**.

If you agree to the terms set forth above, please execute and date this engagement letter and return the same to me. Retain the enclosed copy for your records.

Signature block of the engaging lawyer and date.

Read and Accepted by:

Signature block of the litigation consultant and date.

Appendix D

SAMPLE EXPERT REPORT OF ALLISON P. WAINWRIGHT

Clover Leaf Hedge Fund vs. Crimson Bank & Investment Group, Inc.

Civil Case No. 10-1234

**United States District Court
for the
Name of Venue**

Date

REPORT OF ALLISON P. WAINWRIGHT

Date

I. <u>EXPERT'S QUALIFICATIONS</u>

A. Work experience.

B. Education.

II. <u>SCOPE OF ENGAGEMEMENT</u>

A. Persons involved in the matter.

B. Business relationships.

C. Federal regulatory licensing requirements.

D. Misconducts identified.

E. Monetary damages calculated.

III. **MATERIALS CONSULTED AND RELIED UPON TO MAKE FINDINGS, REACH <u>OPINIONS AND DRAW CONCLUSIONS</u>**

A. Complaint.

B. Response to the complaint.

C. Swap and Derivative Agreements.

D. Counterparty agreements.

E. Bank statements.

F. Insurance company policies which insured the performance of the swap and derivative transactions.

G. Stock brokerage firm account statements.

H. Contracts.

I. Employment agreements.

J. Policy statements.

K. Employee handbook.

L. Risk management guidelines.

M. Clearing agreements.

N. Internal compliance audit reports.

O. External compliance audit reports.

P. Tax returns (corporate and individual).

Q. Testimony of parties archived in deposition transcripts.

IV. **SUMMARY OF FINDINGS**

A. Restate the complaint.

B. Admission to allegation(s).

C. Denial of allegation(s).

D. Provide support for (B) and (C).

V. SUMMARY OF OPINIONS AND CONCLUSIONS

A. *Opinions* are formulated and based on an analysis and review of the above materials - (restate those pertinent documents identified above).

B. *Conclusions* are based on *Findings* made and *Opinions* formulated based on document review and analysis performed.

VI. OVERVIEW OF EVENTS

A. Applicable Federal regulatory impacts.

B. Selected rules, customs, standards and practices of the industry.

VII. BACKGROUND

A. Overview of **Plaintiff's** business.

B. Relationship between **Plaintiff** and **Defendant**.

VIII. ANALYSIS OF THE DEVELOPMENTS CENTRAL TO THE THEME STATED IN THE COMPLAINT

A. What the *Plaintiff* did or did not do.

B. What the *Defendant* did or did not do.

C. Identify actions that caused or prevented harm as the case may be.

D. Explain how applicable industry rules and customs of practice were violated, or not violated as the case may be. Discuss related impacts central to the injuries and damages stated in the *Complaint*.

IX. <u>FINDINGS AND OPINIONS</u>

A. The failure, or the positive application (as the case may be) of internal controls and procedures programs in place to protect against financial loss.

B. The failure to, or the positive action taken (as the case may be) to supervise investment activities.

C. The resulting injury identified, or not injury plausible (as the case may be).

X. <u>CONCLUSION</u>

A. Damages and restitution presented.

B. No damages, the case should be dismissed (as the case may be).

<u>APPENDICES</u>

A. Charts.

B. Graphs.

C. Tables.

BIBLIOGRAPHY

A. Textbooks.

B. Journal articles.

C. Professional magazine articles.

D. Academic studies.

Appendix E

Litigation Forums, Legal and Regulatory Reference Listing

American Arbitration Association (AAA)
140 West 51st Street
New York, New York 10020

Financial Industry Regulatory Authority (FINRA)
Dispute Resolution
1735 K Street, N.W.
Washington, D.C. 20006

Martindale – Hubbell Directory
121 Chanlon Road
New Providence, New Jersey 07974

National Futures Association (NFA)
Dispute Resolution
200 West Madison Street
Suite 1600
Chicago, Illinois 60606

U.S. Commodity Futures Trading Commission (CFTC)
Office of Proceedings
Three Lafayette Centre
1155 21st Street, N.W.
Washington, D.C. 20581

U.S. Securities and Exchange Commission (SEC)
450 Fifth Street, N.W.
Washington, D.C. 20549

Appendix F

United States District Court
Southern District of New York
89 Civ. 2526 (JFK)

Samuel Peltz
Plaintiff

vs.

SHB Commodities, Inc.
Isaac Mayer, Solomon Mayer and Bezalel Mayer
Defendants.

For the Plaintiff:

Herzfeld & Rubin
40 Wall Street
New York, New York 1005

For the Defendant:

Gusrae, Kaplan & Bruno
120 Wall Street
New York, New York 10005

Appendix G

U.S. Commodity Futures Trading Commission
vs.
Anthony Dizona, *et al.*
Civil Action H-05-332.

Appendix H

U.S. Commodity Futures Trading Commission
vs.
Todd J. Delay.
Civil Action 05CV5619.

Appendix I

U.S. Commodity Futures Trading Commission
vs.
Cromwell Financial Services, Inc., *et al.*
Civil Action 05CV210-JD

Glossary of Selected Terms

ABCP – Asset Backed Commercial Paper are short-term loans, ranging from one to six months, typically issued by *SIVs* in which investors have first claim on the *Asset Backed Securities* that the SIV has invested in.[107]

Adversary – an opponent.

Affidavit – is a written statement confirmed by oath or affirmation for use as evidence in court.

Arbitrage CDO – A CDO in which the main motive is arbitrage – to take advantage of a price differential in an asset. In the context of CDOs, an arbitrage is attained by creating a CDO which has returns which are lower than the returns of the underlying assets in the portfolio. The difference is the profit – or the arbitrage – in the deal.[108]

Associated Person (AP) – A person associated with any futures commission merchant, introducing broker, commodity trading advisor, commodity pool operator, or leverage transaction merchant as a partner, officer, employee, consultant or agent. Also, any person occupying similar status or performing similar functions, in any capacity that involves: (a) the solicitation or acceptance of customers' orders. Discretionary accounts, or participation in a commodity pool (other than in a clerical capacity); or (b) the supervision of any person or persons so engaged.[109]

CDO – Collateralised Debt Obligations are *securitizations* of a portfolio of assets into *tranches* with different levels of risk. The equity tranche is

---

107 Ishikawa, p.345.
108 Ibid, p. 346.
109 *The CFTC Glossary*, p. 2.

the most risky as it takes the first losses on the portfolio, but it also has the greatest rate of return. Tranches that take the losses after the equity tranche are often rated by the *rating agencies* – the safest being the AAA-rated tranche which also has the lowest rate of return.[110]

CDS – Credit Default Swaps are market standard insurance contracts on loans or bonds issued by a company (or sovereign nation). If the company which has borrowed money through a loan or bond is unable to pay back and defaults, then the CDS will pay out the original investment amount to the loan – or bond-holder.[111]

Churning – Excessive trading of an account by a broker with control of the account for the purpose of generating commissions while disregarding the interests of the customer.[112]

COMEX – Commodity Exchange, Inc.[113]

Commodity Futures Trading Commission (CFTC) – The Federal regulatory agency established by the CFTC Act of 1974 to administer the Commodity Exchange Act.[114]

Court – a body of people before whom judicial cases are heard; the place where they meet.[115]

CRE CDO – Commercial Real Estate CDOs, backed by a portfolio of commercial mortgages or CMBs.[116]

Curriculum Vitae – a brief account of a person's education, qualifications, and previous occupations, typically sent with a job application.[117]

---

110   Ishikawa, pp. 346-347.
111   Ibid, p. 347.
112   *The CFTC Glossary*, p. 10.
113   The *Futures and Options Course*. Washington, DC: Futures Industry Institute, November 1995, p. 273.
114   *The CFTC Glossary*, p.13.
115   Pearsall, Judy. (ed.). *The Concise Oxford Dictionary*. Oxford: Oxford University Press, 1999, p. 328.
116   Ishikawa, p. 349.
117   Pearsall, p. 352.

Declaration – is an affirmation made instead of taking an oath, usually in writing.

Defendant – an individual, company, or institution sued or accused in a court of law. Also sometimes referred to as respondent.[118]

Derivative – is a financial instrument, traded on or off an exchange, the price of which is directly dependent upon (i.e., 'derived from') the value of one or more underlying securities, equity indices, debt instruments, commodities, other derivative instruments, or any agreed upon pricing index or arrangement (e.g., the movement over time of the Consumer Price Index or freight rates). Derivatives involve the trading of rights or obligations based on the underlying product, but do not directly transfer property. They are used to hedge risk or to exchange a floating rate of return for a fixed rate of return.[119]

Engagement Letter – is a legal document crafted by an attorney to be executed by a litigation consultant or expert witness involving a lawsuit. The engagement letter formally contracts a litigation consultant or expert witness to do certain work associated with later making oral testimony at deposition and trial. The engagement letter provides for payment of litigation consulting and expert witness fees.[120]

Expert Report – is a comprehensive written document used by Expert Witnesses to provide oral testimony at deposition and trials. In addition to the narrative, visual aids such as exhibits, tables and graphs often become a part of the Expert Report. Note: the Expert Report does not include **work product** as defined below. Work product is used to develop the Expert Report.[121]

Futures Commission Merchant (or FCM) – Individuals, associations, partnerships, corporations and trusts that solicit or accept orders for the purchase or sale of any commodity for future delivery on or subject to

---

118   Ibid, p. 375.
119   *The CFTC Glossary*, pp. 20-21.
120   Appendix C.
121   Appendix D.

the rules of any contract market and that accept payment from or extend credit to those whose orders are accepted.[122]

Hedging – Taking a position in a futures market opposite to a position held in the cash market to minimize the risk of financial loss from an adverse price change; a purchase or sale of futures as a temporary substitute for a cash transaction that will occur later.[123]

Introducing Broker (or IB) – Any person (other than a person registered as an "associated person" of a futures commission merchant) who is engaged in soliciting or in accepting orders for the purchase or sale of any commodity for future delivery on an exchange who does not accept any money, securities, or property to margin, guarantee, or secure any trades or contracts that result there from.[124]

Insider trading – Legal insider trading are transactions by insiders and made public by filing a Form 4 with the SEC. Illegal insider trading are trades made by insiders in their company's stock and based on material *non-public* information. These transactions are considered to be *fraudulent*.

Leverage – Finance another term for **gearing.** Use borrowed capital for (an investment) expecting the profits made to be greater than the interest payable.[125]

Litigation – go to law; be a party to a lawsuit, take (a dispute) to a law court.[126]

Litigation Consultant – A person who is expert in a particular field and provides consultant services to counsel who represents a party(s) in a lawsuit. The litigation consultant's duties include such things as education, training, and assistance in case formulation. It does not contemplate giving oral testimony at deposition or trial.

---

122 *The CFTC Glossary*, pp. 28-29.
123 Ibid p. 32.
124 Ibid, p. 34.
125 Pearsall, p. 816.
126 Ibid, p. 829.

National Futures Association (NFA) – A self regulatory organization, composed of futures commission merchants, commodity pool operators, commodity trading advisors, introducing brokers, leverage transaction merchants, commodity exchanges, commercial firms, and banks, that is responsible--under the CFTC oversight—for certain aspects of the regulation of FCMs, CPOs, IBs, LTMs, and their associated persons, focusing primarily on the qualifications and proficiency, financial condition, retail sales practices, and business conduct of these futures professionals.[127]

Negligence – failure to take proper care over something. In *law*, breach of duty of care which results in damage.[128]

Non-testifying Witness – This term is synonymous with litigation consultant.

Plaintiff – a person who brings a case against another in a court of law. Also sometimes referred to as claimant.[129]

Proprietary trading – the market activity of a bank or stock brokerage firm engaged in speculative trading for their own account.

Single-tranche CDO – A CDO in which just one *tranche* can be created on its own, without having to create all the other tranches.[130]

SIV – Structured Investment Vehicles came into existence in the 1990s with the simple business model of using short-term borrowing through the *ABCP* market which they kept rolling over to invest in long-term assets, thereby getting enhanced returns.[131]

---

127 Ibid, p. 41.
128 Ibid, p. 954.
129 Ibid, p. 1092.
130 Ishikawa, p. 355.
131 Ibid.

Speculator – In commodity futures, an individual who does not hedge, but who trades with the objective of achieving profits through the successful anticipation of price movements.[132]

SPV – A Special Purpose Vehicle is a bankruptcy-remote company that is often set up to facilitate a trade. It serves no other function, not even to make a profit.[133]

Subpoena – a writ ordering a person to attend a court.[134]

Swap – is the exchange of one asset or liability for a similar asset or liability for a similar asset or liability for the purpose of lengthening or shortening maturities, or raising or lowering coupon rates, to maximize revenue or minimize financing costs. In securities, this may entail selling one issue and buying another, in foreign currency, it may entail buying a currency on the spot market and simultaneously selling it forward. Swaps may also involve exchange income flows; for example, exchanging the fixed rate coupon stream, or vice versa, while not swapping the principal component of the bond.[135]

Synthetic CDO – A CDO in which the underlying portfolio consists not of the actual assets but of CDS contracts which transfer the risk synthetically.[136]

Testifying Witness (Expert Witness) – A person who has been retained by counsel to provide oral testimony at deposition and trial. This person may have been retained initially as a litigation consultant. Should the litigation consultant role evolve whereby the decision is made to have the consultant testify at deposition and trial, then a revised Engagement Letter must be executed. This is for the purpose of protecting work product *privilege*.

---

132   *The CFTC Glossary*, p. 56.
133   Ishikawa, p. 355.
134   Pearsall, p. 1428.
135   *The CFTC Glossary*, pp.58-59.
136   Ishikawa, p. 355.

Tranche – The term used to describe the individual securities with different risks that are carved out from the repackaging of a portfolio of assets. In an *MBS* (Mortgage backed security) deal, the mortgages *securitized* will be sold in a number of differently-rated tranches. In a CDO, the underlying assets repackaged into securities will be sold in a similar manner.[137]

Unauthorized trading – The entering of a buy or sell trade in a customer's account by a broker who does not have control over the customers account, and has not obtained permission first from the customer to enter those trading transactions.

Work Product – are those materials which are developed during the litigation consulting process. These materials are also used to write an Expert Report. They include, but are not limited to, such things as: 1) hand written notes, 2) e-mails, 3) preliminary analysis, 4) communications with parties pertinent to the case, 5) draft narratives, 6) preliminary findings, conclusions and recommendations as well as 7) draft exhibits. In general, they are items used to develop your Expert Report in preparation to give oral testimony at deposition and trial. Work product does **NOT** include the Expert Report itself.

---

137   Ibid, p. 356.

Bibliography

Adler, Alfred. *The Individual Psychology of Alfred Adler.* New York: Harper Torchbooks, 1964.

Alighieri, Dante. *Inferno.* Oxford: Oxford University Press, 1996.

Amory, Cleveland. *Who Killed Society?* New York: Harper & Brothers Publishers, 1960.

Arkes, Hadley. *First Things.* Princeton: Princeton University Press, 1986.

Baer, Gregory and Gensler, Gary. *The Great Mutual Fund Trap.* New York: Broadway Books, 2002.

Baltzell, E. Digby. *Philadelphia Gentlemen.* Glencoe: The Free Press, 1958.

Barron's. April 13, 2009.

Blumenthal, Robin G. Taking Aim at the Brokers. *Barron's.* October 19, 2009.

Brooks, Ann. *Postfeminisms.* London: Routledge. 1997.

Carroll, Lewis. *Alice's Adventures in Wonderland and Through the Looking-Glass.* New York: Barnes & Noble Classics, 2004.

Cave, Damien. Fraud Accusations Against Florida Lawyer Set Off a Race to Return His Donations. *The New York Times.* November 4, 2009.

Cavender, Nancy M. and Kahane, Howard. *Logic and Contemporary Rhetoric*. Belmont: Wadsworth, CENGAGE Learning, 2010.

Chaucer, Geoffrey. *The Canterbury Tales*. New York: Barnes & Noble Classics, 2006.

Concepcion, Natasha. *Civil Procedure*. New York: Barnes & Noble Publishing, 2003.

Cooke, John William. *Generations of Style*. New York: Brooks Brothers, Inc., 2003.

Debtor-creditor.lawyers.com 9/13/2009.

Efrati, Amir. U.S. Loses Bear Fraud Case. *The Wall Street Journal*. November 11, 2009.

Futures and Options Course. Washington, DC: Futures Industry Institute, November 1995.

Grady, Allison. Daubert and Expert testimony. *Virtual Mentor*. Volume 8, Number 2: 97-100. February 2006.

Hall, Kevin G. New Rules to Affect Valuation of Toxic Assets. San Diego: *Union-Tribune*. April 2, 2009.

Henriques, Diana B. Plea From Madoff Accountant May Lead to Tax Cases. *The New York Times*. November 4, 2009.

Ishikawa, Tetsuya. *How I Caused the Credit Crunch*. London: Icon Books Ltd., 2009.

Manuet, Thomas A. *Fundamentals of Trial Techniques*. Boston: Little Brown & Company, 1992.

McCoy, Kevin and Petrecca, Laura. Insider trading bust digs deep. *USA Today*. November 6, 2009.

Meltzer, Allan H. *A History of the Federal Reserve. Volume 1*: 1913-1951. Chicago: The University of Chicago Press, 2003.

Milton, John. *Paradise Lost.* Mineola: Dover Publications, Inc., 2005.

Morgenson, Gretchen and Story, Louise. Banks Bundled debt. Bet Against It and Won. *The New York Times.* December 24, 2009.

Norris, Frank. *The Octopus.* Boston: Houghton Mifflin, 1958.

Office of Public Affairs: Commodity Futures Trading Commission. *The CFTC Glossary.* Washington, DC: CFTC Publications, 1992.

Pearsall, Judy. (ed.). *The Concise Oxford Dictionary.* Oxford: Oxford University Press, 1999.

Pojman, Louis P. and Vaughn, Lewis. *Philosophy: The Quest for Truth.* New York: Oxford University Press, 2009.

Rawls, John. *A Theory of Justice.* Cambridge: Harvard University Press, 1971.

Rawls, John. *Political Liberalism.* New York: Columbia University Press, 1996.

Shakespeare, William. *Hamlet.* New York: Barnes & Noble Classics, 2003.

Sorkin, Andrew Ross. *Too Big to Fail.* New York: Penguin Group, 2009.

Soros, George. *The Crash of 2008 and What it Means.* New York: PublicAffairs, 2009.

Sullivan, Tom. Hedge Funds Underperform This Year. *Barron's.* October 26, 2009.

The Avalon Project: Washington's Farewell Address 1796 last modified on: 02/02/2008. Copyright 1996 The Avalon Project at Yale Law School.

The Book *of* Common Prayer. According to the use of *The Episcopal Church*. New York: The Church Hymnal Corporation, 1979.

The Economist. A new sheriff. Washington, DC: September 5th-11th 2009.

The Economist. Papandreou tries to prop up the pillars. December 19th 2009 – January 1st 2010.

The Economist. Dubai's debt cliffhanger. December 19th 2009 – January 1st 2010.

Turabian, Kate L. *A Manual for Writers of Term Papers, Theses, and Dissertations*. Chicago: The University of Chicago Press, 1996.

Vanderbilt, Amy. *Amy Vanderbilt's Etiquette*. Garden City: Doubleday & Company, 1972.

Wei, Lingling and Grant, Peter. Banks Hasten to Adopt New Rules. *The Wall Street Journal*. November 11, 2009.

www.bis.org/statistics/derstata.htm.

www.usdoj.gov. 8/4/2009.

www.worldbank.org.

Index

A

Ad hominem 22, 33, 34
Adler, Alfred 88, 115
Administrative Law Judge 8
Affidavit 45, 51
Alice's Adventures in Wonderland and Through the Looking-Glass 66, 115
Alighieri, Dante 73, 115
Alternative Dispute Resolution 11
American Arbitration Association (AAA) 1, 11, 96, 103
Amory, Cleveland 87
Amy Vanderbilt's Etiquette (Vanderbilt) 33, 73, 118
A new sheriff (The Economist) 2, 118
Arbitration ix, xiv, 1, 9, 11, 12, 13, 14, 18, 19, 20, 22, 26, 33, 38, 60, 63, 71, 73, 74, 77, 78, 96
Arkes, Hadley 57, 115
Asset Backed Commercial Paper 108
Associated Person (AP) 108
Avalon Project, the 74, 118
Awards 37, 92

B

Baer, Gregory 2, 115
Baltzell, E. Digby 71, 115
Bank for International Settlements (BIS) 85
Bank of the United States 84
Banks Hasten to Adopt New Rules (Wei) 89, 118
Barron's 12, 85, 86, 115, 117
Bear Stearns 2, 84
Blackmun, Harry Supreme Court Justice 51, 52
Blumenthal, Robin G. 12, 115
Book of Common Prayer, the 59, 118
Brooks, Ann (Postfeminisms) 88

C

Canterbury, Tales the (Chaucer) 9, 116
Carroll, Lewis 66, 115
Case formulation 9, 30, 31, 45, 62, 68, 111
Cash market 3, 111
Cave, Damien 86, 115
Cavender, Nancy M. 33, 87, 116
Chaucer, Geoffrey 9, 116
Churning 2
Civil Procedure 42, 116
COMEX 15, 46, 61, 109
Commodity futures industry 2, 3
Commodity Futures Trading Commission, U.S. (CFTC) 2, 11, 83, 103, 105, 106, 107, 109, 117, 125
Compensation 15, 31, 88, 93
Concepcion, Natasha (Civil Procedure) 42, 116
Concise Oxford Dictionary, the 109, 117
Conferences 24, 26, 37, 39, 78
Confidentiality 42, 95
Construction industry, lawsuits 1, 30
Cooke, John William 23, 24, 116
Corporate misconduct 5
Corruption, corrupt 88

Court, courtroom xiv, 11, 12, 13, 18, 20, 22, 24, 33, 34, 35, 36, 38, 43, 45, 51, 52, 59, 61, 62, 64, 65, 70, 71, 73, 78, 79, 80, 86, 94, 95, 108, 110, 111, 112, 113

Crash of 2008 and what it Means, the (Soros) 3, 88, 92, 117

Credit Default Swaps (CDS) 3

Criminal matters 7, 15, 69, 77

Cross-examination 23, 56, 59, 60, 61, 63, 64, 67, 73

Curriculum Vitae xiii, 29, 33, 37, 38, 66, 78, 83, 90, 109

Curriculum Vitae Certification Binder 38

D

Daubert and Expert Testimony (Grady) 50

Daubert, William 51

Declaration 110

Defendant 7, 14, 69, 100, 104, 110

Deposition xi, xiii, xiv, 9, 10, 22, 23, 31, 32, 33, 34, 45, 46, 47, 49, 55, 56, 57, 58, 59, 60, 61, 62, 63, 64, 65, 66, 67, 68, 69, 70, 71, 73, 74, 80, 99, 110, 111, 113, 114

Derivatives 110

Do's and Don'ts at Deposition and Trial 70

Dress code 22, 23

E

Ebbers, Bernard 86

Economics, Division of 19

Economist, The 2, 87, 118

Education 24, 36, 38, 39, 45, 109, 111

Efrati, Amir 89, 116

Enforcement, Division of 8, 13

Engagement Letter 32, 50, 96, 110

Ethics 74, 89

Experience, academic, industry, regulatory xi, xiii, xiv, 1, 2, 3, 4, 8, 9, 11, 12, 13, 14, 16, 17, 18, 19, 20, 23, 24, 25, 26, 29, 30, 34, 35, 36, 37, 38, 39, 45, 46, 47, 49, 51, 62, 67, 72, 75, 77, 78, 86, 97, 98, 100, 101, 109, 112

Expert Report xiii, 29, 31, 43, 45, 46, 47, 49, 50, 51, 52, 53, 55, 57, 59, 60, 62, 63, 64, 65, 67, 68, 70, 71, 74, 79, 80, 83, 110, 114

Expert witness list 61

F

Federal Deposit Insurance Corporation ix, 125

Fee schedule xiii, 29, 30, 32, 42, 50, 79

Financial crisis 2, 12, 85, 88, 89

Financial Industry Regulatory Authority (FINRA) 4, 12, 103

Financial wreckage 87

First Things (Arkes) 57, 115

Fraud 86, 89, 115, 116

Fraud Accusations … (Cave) 86, 115

Fundamentals of Trial Techniques 62, 116

Futures Commission Merchant (FCM) 8, 60, 108, 111

Futures, commodity 2, 11, 12, 83, 103, 105, 106, 107, 109, 110, 112, 116, 117, 125

G

Generations of Style (Cooke) 23, 24, 116

Gensler, Gary 2

Glossary, CFTC 11, 45, 108, 109, 110, 111, 113, 117

Glossary of Selected Terms 108

Goldman Sachs 2

Grady, Allison 50, 77, 116

Grant, Peter 89, 118

Great Depression of the 1930s 84, 85

Great Mutual Fund Trap, the (Gensler) 2, 115
Great Recession of the 21st century 3, 84, 85
Greed 8
Gusrae, Kaplan & Bruno ix, 104

H

Hallberg, Budd J. ix, 15, 125
Hall, Kevin G. 89, 116
Hamlet (Shakespeare) 73, 117
Harvard University 17, 117, 125
Hedge Funds Underperform This Year (Sullivan) 86, 117
Hedge, hedging 86, 92, 97, 117
Henriques, Diana B. 86, 116
Hirshauer, Ph.D., V. Bruce ix
History of the Federal Reserve, A (Meltzer) 84, 117
Hot Seat, Tales from the 38, 59, 60, 62, 65, 68, 70
Housing bubble, U.S. 4
How I Caused the Credit Crunch 4, 116

I

Individual Psychology of Alfred Adler (Adler) 88, 115
Inferno (Alighieri) 73, 115
Inside information 87
Insider trading 87, 111, 116
Insider trading bust digs deep (McCoy) 87, 111, 116
Internet 1, 4, 26
Ishikawa, Tetsuya 4

J

Joyce, Ph.D., Thomas ix
Judgment proof 65, 66
Jury 5, 7, 8, 9, 14, 19, 20, 21, 22, 23, 24, 26, 34, 36, 52, 61, 62, 63, 64, 68, 70, 72, 74, 77, 78, 80
Justice as fairness 8, 17, 18

K

Kahane, Howard 33, 116
Kant, Immanuel 17, 89

L

Lambert & Weiss ix
Law firms ix, 25, 26, 79, 80
Lefcourt, Esq., Gerald B. ix
Lehman Brothers 3, 84
Litigation ix, xi, xiii, xiv, 1, 2, 4, 5, 7, 8, 9, 11, 12, 13, 14, 15, 16, 18, 20, 24, 25, 26, 27, 29, 30, 31, 34, 35, 41, 42, 45, 46, 50, 51, 61, 64, 65, 68, 69, 70, 72, 73, 74, 77, 78, 79, 81, 88, 89, 94, 96, 110, 111, 112, 113, 114, 125
Litigation consultant xi, xiii, xiv, 1, 5, 8, 9, 11, 12, 13, 14, 15, 16, 24, 27, 29, 30, 31, 34, 41, 45, 46, 65, 69, 70, 72, 74, 77, 79, 81, 94, 96, 110, 111, 112, 113, 125
Litigation forums 7
Litigation portfolio 9

M

Madoff, Bernard L. 8, 15, 86, 116
Manual for Writers of Term Papers, Theses and Dissertations, A (Turabian) 37, 118
Manuet, Thomas A. 62, 116
Marketing Plan 26
Martindale-Hubbell Directory 63
McCoy, Kevin 87
Mediation 11, 12
Medical field 1
Meltzer, Allan H. 84, 117
Merrill Lynch Pierce Fenner & Smith ix
Military experience 36
Misconduct 2, 5, 78
Moral, fortitude, high ground, standard 17, 70, 73, 74, 79, 81, 87

Morgan JP 2, 84
Morgenson, Gretchen (Banks Bundled debt, Bet Against It and Won) 4

N

National Futures Association (NFA) 12, 103, 112
Negligence 112
New Rules to Affect Valuation of Toxic Assets (Hall) 89, 116
Newspapers and periodicals 37
New York Stock Exchange, the ix, 125
Non-testifying expert xiv, 41, 69
Norris, Frank 3

O

Octopus, The (Norris) 3, 117
Overtolerance 87

P

Paradise Lost 24, 117
Pearsall, Judy 109, 111, 113, 117
Peer review 49
Perkins Coie ix
Peterson, Lacy, In the Matter of 8
Petrecca, Laura 87, 116
Philadelphia Gentlemen (Baltzell) 71, 115
Philosophy: The Quest for Truth (Pojman) 17, 117
Plaintiff 1, 7, 69, 100, 104, 112
Plea from Madoff Accountant ... (Henriques) 86, 116
Pojman, Louis P. 17, 89, 117
Political liberalism 18, 117
Ponzi scheme 15, 86
Postfeminisms 88
Professional development, experience 36, 91
Progressive Era 3
Proskauer Rose ix
Psalm 19:2 59
Publications 11, 24, 117

R

Rawls, John 17
Real estate 1, 3, 4, 35, 78, 85
Reed Smith Shaw & McClay ix
Reparations 11
Retainer, retained 31
Rosch & Ross ix

S

Securities 1, 2, 4, 12, 13, 19, 25, 30, 35, 72, 86, 110, 111, 113, 114
Securities and Exchange Commission, U.S. (SEC) 4, 13, 103
Self Regulatory Organization (SRO) 112
Shakespeare, William 73, 117
Sidley Austin, Brown & Wood ix
Single-tranche CDO 112
Skilling, Jeffrey 86
Smith Barney, Inc. ix
Sorkin, Andrew Ross 3, 5, 117
Soros, George 84, 85
Speciale, Esq. CPA, Raymond C. ix
Special Purpose Vehicle (SPV) 113
Speculate, speculation 3
Stock brokerage 2, 12, 25, 78, 85, 112
Subpoena 113
Sullivan, Tom 86, 117
Super-Bubble 3
Superiority complex (Adler) 88
Sutherland, Asbill & Brennan ix
Swaps 3, 72, 85
Synthetic CDO 113

T

Taking Aim at the Brokers (Blumenthal) 12, 115
Telecommunications 1, 4
Testifying expert xiv, 41, 56, 69

Testimony, direct, expert, oral, written xiii, 4, 5, 9, 10, 11, 12, 14, 18, 19, 20, 22, 23, 29, 30, 31, 32, 33, 34, 38, 45, 46, 47, 49, 50, 51, 52, 55, 56, 57, 59, 60, 62, 63, 64, 65, 67, 68, 69, 70, 71, 72, 73, 74, 77, 78, 79, 80, 110, 111, 113, 114, 116

Theory of Justice, A (Rawls) 17, 18, 117

Too Big to Fail (Sorkin) 3, 5, 88, 117

Tranche 108, 109, 112

Trial xi, xiii, xiv, 10, 11, 14, 21, 22, 23, 24, 25, 26, 27, 31, 32, 41, 42, 45, 46, 51, 52, 55, 56, 57, 59, 60, 61, 62, 63, 64, 65, 66, 67, 68, 69, 70, 71, 73, 74, 77, 78, 79, 80, 110, 111, 113, 114

Turabian, Kate L. 37, 118

U

Unauthorized trading 2

U.S. Loses Bear Fraud Case (Efrati) 89, 116

V

Vanderbilt, Amy 33, 73, 118

Vaughn, Lewis 17, 117

Victim 9

W

Wakefield, Esq., Susannah J. ix

Wall Street Journal 89, 116, 118

Wei, Lingling 89, 118

Who Killed Society? (Amory) 87, 115

Work Product 41, 42, 43, 45, 49, 51, 52, 65, 70, 79, 94, 95, 110, 113

World Bank, the 85

www.usdoj.gov 86, 118

About The Author

Budd Hallberg started his career in 1966 as an investment banker, first with Francis I. duPont & Company, then Dominick & Dominick, Inc., and later Hornblower & Weeks-Hemphill, Noyes, Inc. He was a member of the New York Coffee, Sugar and Cocoa Exchange, the New York Cotton Exchange and the New York Mercantile Exchange in New York City.

In 1976, Hallberg joined the U.S. Commodity Futures Trading Commission (CFTC) in Washington, D.C. In 1979, the CFTC awarded him the Federal government's Meritorious Service Award. He was appointed a Director of the agency that same year.

Hallberg is an internationally respected litigation consultant and expert witness. Beginning in 1985, his litigation career spanned a period of 23 years and involved 43 lawsuits. He acted as a testifying witness in 26 of those 43 cases. Hallberg provided litigation consultant and expert witness services to organizations such as the Federal Deposit Insurance Corporation, Merrill Lynch, Pierce, Fenner and Smith and the New York Stock Exchange. He is a member of the Chartered Financial Analyst Society of Philadelphia.

In 1965, Hallberg was appointed a Reserve Commissioned Officer in the Army of the United States. He is a graduate of the Command and General Staff College of the United States Army. Hallberg is the recipient of the Meritorious Service Medal and the Army Commendation Medal with two Oak Leaf Clusters. He retired from the United States Army with the rank of Lieutenant Colonel in 2002.

Hallberg has a B.S. degree in liberal studies from the University of the State of New York. He holds a M.A. degree in philosophy from Goddard College. Hallberg also studied at the University of Connecticut and Harvard University.

He is a member of the Racquet Club of Philadelphia and the Society of the Cincinnati. Hallberg is an avid horseback rider and enjoys golf and tennis.

Made in the USA
Lexington, KY
29 March 2012